Édouard Jules Corroyer

Descriptive guide of Mont Saint-Michel

Édouard Jules Corroyer
Descriptive guide of Mont Saint-Michel
ISBN/EAN: 9783337336363
Printed in Europe, USA, Canada, Australia, Japan
Cover: Foto ©Lupo / pixelio.de

More available books at **www.hansebooks.com**

DESCRIPTIVE GUIDE

OF

MONT SAINT-MICHEL

By ÉDOUARD CORROYER

ARCHITECT TO THE GOVERNMENT

PARIS

GENERAL LIBRARY OF ARCHITECTURE AND OF PUBLIC WORKS

DUCHER ET CIE

51, RUE DES ÉCOLES, 51

1883

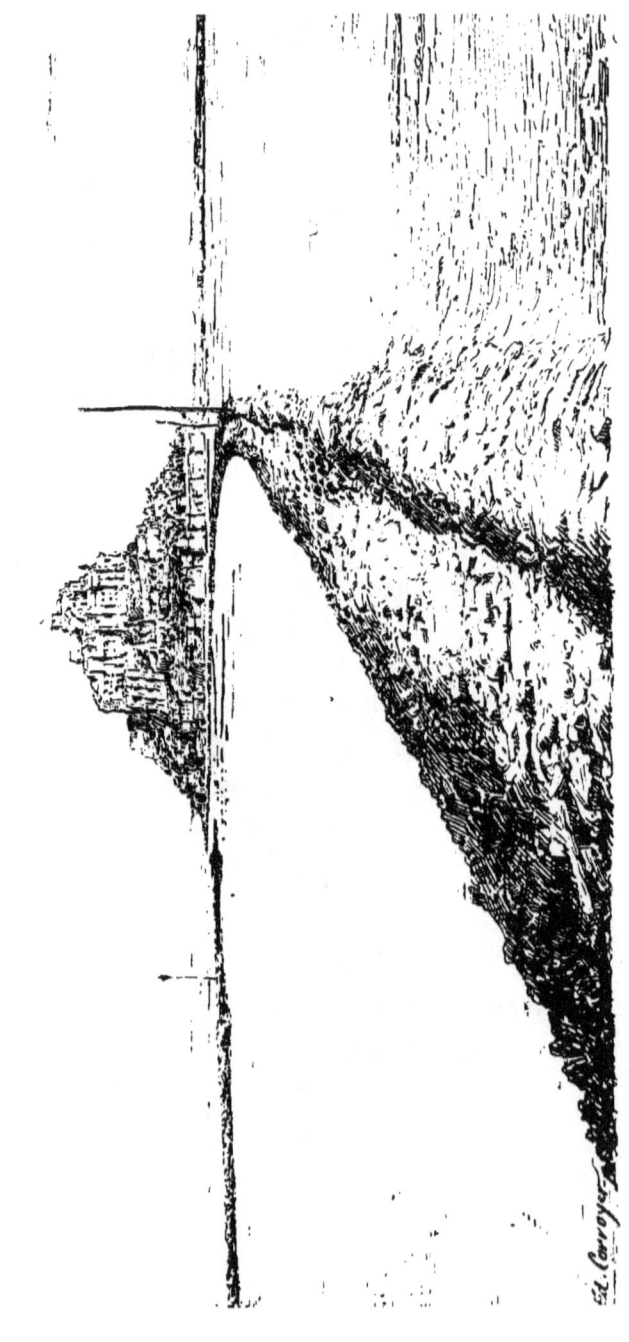

HISTORICAL NOTICE

1.

Fig. 3.
Stamp of pilgrimage found at Mont Saint-Michel.

DESCRIPTIVE GUIDE

OF

MONT SAINT-MICHEL[1]

HISTORICAL NOTICE

The rock which rises majestically in the middle of the immense estuary extending from the coasts of Normandy on the north to those of Britanny on the south and the sea on the north-west has been called Mont Saint-Michel from the eighth century.

There does not exist on the old rock any construction built before the eleventh century, therefore there is no proof of the existence of buildings erected before that time.

---

(1) Quoted partly from a book of the author: *The description of the Abbey of Mont Saint-Michel and its environs preceded by an historical notice*, Paris, 1877. This work has been subscribed to by the Minister of public instruction and fine arts, and crowned by the Institute, the Academy of inscriptions et belles-lettres. Concourse of the national antiquities of 1878.

However, having respect to the old traditions which are to be taken into account it is interesting to call to mind some parts of Dom Jean Huynes's (1) writings, relating to the foundation of the primitive sanctuary erected by Saint-Aubert in honour of the archangel Saint-Michel, as well as the principal events which happened during the first period of the existence of the Abbey, *i. e.* from the beginning of the eighth to the end of the eleventh century.

According to the author, Saint-Aubert, a bishop of Avranches erected, at the commencement of the eighth century a church in honour of Saint-Michel who had appeared to him several times in his dreams: « ... In 708, Saint-Aubert who had overcome, with the help of God, all the difficulties attending the building of his church, and who knew the dimensions which the archangel Saint-Michel wished, worked at it himself. He did not build it magnificently nor with great art, but he gave it the form of a grotto wishing it to be like the church which the glorious Saint-Michel had dug himself in the rock of Mont-Gargan, and desiring to intimate by these means that God does not ask for splendour and magnificence in visible temples but from our hearts which are the temples of the Holy Spirit... »

After the consecration of the chapel on the sixteenth of october 709, Saint-Aubert founded the Abbey of Mont Saint-Michel by establishing a college of twelve clerks or canons to celebrate divine service. . He conferred on them goods and chattels sufficient for their food and clothing, and added the villages of Huynes and Genest for that same purpose.

1) *General history of the Abbey of MontSaint-Michel called the peril of the sea, diocese of Avranches, province of Normandy*, etc. National library, french fonts, n°' 18917 and 18918.

Having thus provided for the necessities of the canons by these means, there remained a difficulty about the water supply, for during his life he had found there was always a scarcity of fresh water on the mountain. Therefore he and those who were with him began to pray and implore our lord through the intercession of the archangel Saint-Michel to show them a fountain of fresh water, as they would serve him henceforth in that place... The archangel appeared to the bishop and showed him at the foot of the rock a fountain at which not only have thirsty ones quenched their thirst, but also at which many infirm and fever striken persons, after drinking the water, have recovered their health. From that time the fountain was called Saint-Aubert, and it was used until cisterns were invented... It is surrounded by a high tower. On going down to the lower rooms under the cloister, one can see a large flight of steps closed in by walls on either side and by which the former inhabitants went down from the monastery to draw water...

« The apparition of the Archangel saint Michel to Saint-Aubert soon spread far and wide. Pilgrims came to visit the Abbey from distant provinces... the pope, the king of France and the Hibernians sent holy relics... The rock was then called the Mont Saint-Michel and surnamed the peril of the sea, not because the sea dashes idly against it, but because the ebb and flow washing away on the shingle the paths to it cause them to be dangerous to strangers... » (don Jean Huynes).

The celebrity of the Mont Saint-Michel increased until the end of the ninth century; but after the death of Charlemagne, the Normans invaded his dismembered empire, and having as their cheif the formidable Rollo surnamed the Walker, they devastated western Neustria. From this time dates the origin of the town which still exists, and which was established by some homeless families looking for a shelter on the Mont Saint-Michel.

In the tenth century Rollo made peace, at Saint-Clair-sur-Epte, with king Charles-the-Simple. This prince gave him his daughter Giselle and the province of Neustria which the new duke named Normandy.

In 966, Rollo's grandson, Richard-sans-Peur, established on Mont Saint-Michel the benedictine monks who, from Mount-Cassin (where about 529 saint Benoit had established their first monastery) overspread all Europe and became the most justly celebrated of the monks of that time.

Richard II, duke of Normandy, son of Richard-sans-Peur, founded in 1020 the church of which the transepts and four arcades of the nave are still existing (1).

Hildebert II, fourth abbot from 1017 to 1023, was « entrusted by Richard with the details of the works; he paid particular attention to the foundation... » (de Gerville).

After many vicissitudes, the church commenced in 1020, was finished in 1135 by Bernard « a professed monk of the abbey of the Bec and a prior of Cremont, who ordered a beautiful, high and strong tower to be built on the four large pillars of the chancel... » (don Jean Huynes); the building was not damaged by the fire kindled by the rebel inhabitants of Avranches in 1138, which burnt to the ground the town and the monastery the buildings of which were at that time on the north west of the basilica. After its com-

---

(1) The chancel of the church has been rebuilt in the XVth century and the three first arcades of the nave were destroyed at the end of the XVIIIth century.

pletion, the church was composed of the chancel, the transepts and the nave, having seven arcades, terminated on the west by a front having three doors and over the principal one, a large window lighting the central nave. There was a court in front laid out over the foundations built by Hildebert seconded by Robert de Torigni, after his election, which marked a period of great prosperity for the Abbey. During the thirty-two years this eminent abbot governed it, 1154 to 1186, the study of science, literature and poetry received a considerable impulse. He greatly enlarged the monastery by building the hostelry and the infirmary on the south and on the west, around the Roman works, various buildings joining together the offices from the south to the north, and over which he constructed two towers joined by a porch in front of the romanesque church.

To the end of the XIIth century, the Abbey was not damaged by fires caused by men or by lightning; but the conflagration of 1203 was terrible. Gui de Thouars unable to take the Mont Saint-Michel set the houses of the town on fire; the flames reached the building and every part was burnt down, except the church, the walls and the vaults. The abbots, successors of Robert de Torigni, followed his example not only by raising up again and maintaining the church and the Abbey, but, be it said to their praise, by building the magnificent edifices of the north, named from the beginning the *Merveille* and which were all constructed at one time, thanks to the liberality of Philippe Auguste.

The Merveille was begun in 1203 by Jourdain XVIIth abbot, 1191 to 1212; he built the room of the Almonry, the Cellar and began the Refectory above the Almonry which Raoul des Isles finished from 1212 to 1218. Thomas des

Chambres completed the room of the Chevaliers and the lateral gallery giving more space for walking. He made also at that epoch the Dormitory over the Refectory and finished it before his death which took place in 1225.

He also began the cloister which was finished by Raoul de Villedieu in 12 28. This abbot modified the north front of the transept of the romanesque church and established at its base the *Lavatorium*, in the south Gallery of the Cloister. He built too the lateral portal which opens towards the southern platform — called the Saut-Gaultier — as well as the chapel Saint-Etienne on the south of the romanesque foundations, near the hostelry built by Robert de Torigni.

Up to that time Mont Saint-Michel had no real fortifications. The Abbey and the houses grouped at its foot were only protected by stone walls or by palisades. Jourdain and his successors began the defensive works on the north at the same time as the Merveille. Richard Tustin, 21" abbot (1236 to 1264) continued their work. He built the large building, on the east of the church, named Belle-Chaise and the Residence of the Abbot on the south, or at least he began it; he ordered the fortified tower to be erected which surrounded and rose above the fountain Saint-Aubert and joined this tower to the roads by a staircase closed by embattled walls. Thanks to Saint-Louis's generosity, when this king went as a pilgrim to Mont Saint-Michel, about 1256, this abbot was enabled to increase the fortifications of the place, and to order the tower of the North to bebuilt, insuring the defence of the Abbey, the entrance of which he had restored. At last, about 1260, he began, on the western gallery of the Cloister, the Chapter-house, the door alone of which was finished.

In the fourteenth century the fires which brought such ruin to Mont Saint-Michel began again. In July of 1300, the lightning struck the steeple of the church and ruined it entirely, as well as the high towers erected by Robert de Torigni. The bells were melted : the roofs of the church and of several buildings were burnt and the flames spread by a strong wind, communicated the fire to the town which was almost entirely destroyed. Guillaume du Château, XXVe abbot, from 1299 to 1344 helped by the generosity of the pilgrims, repaired the disasters and, thanks to the liberality of king Philippe-le-Bel after a pilgrimage to the mount, he rebuilt the houses of the town and the warehouses of the Abbey, called the *Fanils*, at the foot of the rock on the south-west. He continued the ramparts commenced by Richard Turtin, and appointed the attendant Pierre de Toufou the guardian of the door of the town. During the time of Jean de la Porte (twenty-sixth abbot, from 1314 to 1334), Mont Saint-Michel without garrison until that time, became an important fortress was and held for the king of France.

In 1350, the lightning again struck the church and set fire to the Abbey. Nicolas le Vitrier (1335 to 1362), quickly repaired the damages and kept the ramparts in order, in spite of the continual threats of the English who ravaged at that time the coasts of Normandy; he was the first of the abbots at the same time military and religious governor of the town and of the Abbey, appointed by Charles V who was then only duke of Normandy.

After the death of Nicolas le Vitrier, Geoffroy de Servon, XXVIIIe regular abbot, succeeded to his place and dignity and obtained from king Charles V, in 1364 and 1365, the right to order arms to be given up by every person other than the king and his brothers, entering the Abbey. He ordered numerous works to be done in the church, dormitories and other buildings of this monastery, which, on the 8th of july 1374, were burnt by lightning as well as the whole city.

Pierre le Roy, XXIX*th* abbot, from 1386 to 1411, who succeeded to Geoffroy de Servon, was one of the most celebrated abbots of the Mont Saint-Michel, and with Roger II, Robert de Torigny, Jourdain, regular abbots, and Guillaume d'Estouville, first commandatory abbot, one of the greatest builders and restorers of the Abbey. He rebuilt the top of the tower, so called — of the Corbins, — at the south-east angle and the Merveille — restored and recovered the abbatial buildings, on the south of the church, commenced by Richard Tustin about 1260, continued by his successors and in part ruined by the fire of 1374. He completed the defences of the east by erecting the Perrine tower about the end of the fourteenth century. On the north of Belle-Chaise he built, in the first years of the fifteenth century, the Châtelet and the small curtain which joins it to the Merveille. In order to cover the Châtelet he made the Barbican which surrounds it and also the large flight of steps on the north and modified the ramparts on the north and on the west. The king Charles VI, during a pilgrimage to Mont Saint-Michel, in 1393 confirmed Pierre le Roy in his office of captain of Mont Saint-Michel. Pierre le Roy is the first of the regular abbots who ordered his armorial bearings to be placed on the walls of the Abbey; his coat of arms adorned the chairs or the stalls of the chancel which were restored by his order in 1389; according to the historians of the seventeenth and eighteenth century this abbot had : of *gueules à trois pals d'or, au franc quartier de Bretagne, à la cotice denchée brochant sur le tout.*

Robert Jolivet, XXXth regular abbot, had accompanied Pierre le Roy to the council of Pisa and, when this illustrious abbot died at Bologna in 1411, he obtained from the pope John XXIII the government of the Abbey; he was afterwards elected by the monks and entrusted by the king with the guardianship of the Mount. During the first years of his administration, he seemed inclined to follow the example of his predecessors, but tiring of the severe rule of his Abbey, he studied in the « Faculté des Décrets ». Recalled to his Abbey which was being threatened by the English who had seized upon Normandy in 1415 after the battle of Agincourt, and had fortified themselves in Tombelaine in 1417, Robert Jolivet, though he had forgotten his duties of abbot remembered, at the moment of danger those which he was bound to fulfil as the governor of the fortress. After having collected provisions of all kind, thanks to the resources of the Abbey, and to the assistance which he received from Charles VI, he built around the enlarged town the irregular enclosure which still exists, joined its new fortifications on the east to those erected by Guillaume du Château in the fourteenth century, by extending them on the south and flanking them by six towers. However he soon grew tired of his new military life, and in 1420 he yielded to the splendid offers of the king of England. « He withdrew to Rouen among the English who were masters of this town and of Normandy... By accepting high office under the duke of Bedford, Robert Jolivet incurred the hatred of the monks whose love of their fatherland had remained steadfast. They named a successor to him... » (de Gerville). The abbot Jean Gonault during the absence of his regular abbot courageously governed the Abbey. « In addition to these misfortunes of war, Jean Gonault saw, in 1421, on the eve of Saint-Martin's feast, the whole end of this church even to the stalls in the chancel fall to the ground without, however, any body being injured » (don Jean Huynes).

In 1425, Louis d'Estouteville, military governor of the fortress of the Mount, built the Barbican in front of the gate of the town so as to cover its approaches. The town sustained a long but glorious siege; from 1422 to 1434 it resisted victoriously the assaults of the English. In 1435 they tried a last assault : routed by the garrison and the knights, defenders of the Mount, they abandoned their artillery the bombards of which, now adorning the forepart of the Barbican, second entrance door, remain as curious specimens.

During a period of about thirty years, the Abbey was in the greatest distress; its property being sequestrated, it was obliged to pawn its silver plate, its shrines and its reliquaries, in order to feed the monks, the inhabitants of the town, and the garrison of the fortress. This state of things lasted until 1450, when after the battle of Formigny, the English abandoned Normandy and were driven out of France, — except Calais which they kept until 1558.

As early as 1450, it became possible to undertake the works so much needed by the Abbey and Guillaume d'Estouteville, first commandatory abbot, began the chancel of the church. « He obtained from the popes several bulls containing plenary indulgences... for all who should visit this church of Mont Saint-Michel and give alms. By these means and also with the assistance of the Abbey revenues, they began to rebuild the chancel, which since 1421 was in uins, and to rebuild it not as it was at first, but so sumptuously that if they had continued building the other parts of the church with the same magnificence it would have been impossible to see in France a more beautiful structure » (don Jean Huynes).

The cardinal d'Estouteville however gave up the idea of rebuilding the whole of the church on the same plan, and ordered two arcades to be made joining together the pillars of the central steeple but of a different form from the others. Instead of jointed arches he made buttresses in order to stop the complete ruin of two of the pillars of the triumphal arches which the falling of the romanesque chancel in 1421 had bended and deformed. They are still in that state.

The works were interrupted in 1482 by the cardinal's death. André Laure limited the work to adorning the chapels erected by his predecessor. Guillaume de Lamps ordered the work to be continued... » Besides which, says don Jean Huynes the fire of heaven having burnt the steeple and melted the bells, he ordered all to be rebuilt. » This citation shows that the steeple had been rebuilt with wood after the falling of the stone one built in thet welfth century by Bernard du Bec. According to some authors the wooden spire—rebuilt by Guillaume de Lamps in 1509, was crowned by a golden statue of the Archangel Saint-Michel with unfurled wings...

Jean de Lamps, XXXIV[me] and last regular abbot, 1513 to 1523, recommence dthe works of the chancel, left unfinished since his brother's death, « He ordered the whole of the building which covers the big altar, to be finished even from the top of the first pane of glass. This was done,

2.

panes of glasses, pillars, vaults and roofs were rebuilt as they stand now » (don Jean Huynes). This magnificent chancel, finished in 1521 was the last of the remarkable constructions of Mont Saint-Michel. We may however remark that about 1530, the lieutenant of the king Francis I[st] ordered the tower or bastillon Gabriel to be erected in the place where the mount now is. The name was taken from its author Gabriel du Puy. The object was to complete the defences of the Abbey on the west where the rock can be used. At that time a small work was built near the Barbican of the gate of the town. It formed the *Avancée* of the place and was used as the guardhouse of the burghers of the Mount. The ramparts were altered, principally those of the projecting tower on the east.

The succeeding abbots ceased building, and several of them showed the greatest dislike to keep up the buildings erected by their predecessors. A fire happened in 1564 which burnt a great part of the monastery; five years after no repairs were begun and a decree of the Rouen parliament was necessary to compel the abbot François le Roux to do the necessary works. He being dissatisfied exchanged his Abbey with Arthur de Cossé, bishop of Coutances; the zeal of whom was not greater than that of his predecessor. The cardinal de Joyeuse who succeeded him was not more disposed to make the necessary repairs. In 1594, the lightning fell again on the steeple, burnt a part of its timberwork and that of the church. Other damages were done. Another decree of Parliament was necessary to compel the Abbot to repair these buildings.

During the wars of the Ligue, the abbots of the Mount had too often to protect their Abbey against the attacks of the Huguenots to think of enlarging or even of repairing the buildings. However the decree published by the Rouen parliament, on the 12ᵗʰ of september 1602, forced the general intendants of the Abbey, the sir of Brévent and Jean de Surtainville to erect the massive tower which still exists.

Fivenew bells were put in the steeple.

In 1615, Henri de Lorraine, at the age of five years, was named by Louis XIII the seventh *commendataire*. His father Charles de Lorraine, duke of Guise, ordered repairs in the Abbey to be made in 1616 and, in 1618, in order to strengthen the western part of the buildings erected at the end of the twelfth century, by Robert de Torigni, he ordered a buttress to be made, which cost 14000 pounds; on the top of this buttress one can still see an escutcheon with the Lorraine arms.

During these troubled times, we remark a great relaxation in the customs of the monks; in 1622 the confusion seemed insufferable, and on the 27ᵗʰ october of 1622 they were succeeded by the Benedictine monks of the congregation of Saint-Maur.

The new inhabitants of Mont Saint-Michel kept the buildings from going to ruin but they do not seem to have taken any great care to keep them intact. In 1627, they built a wind mill on the bastillon Gabriel and made many interior changes. Many marks of their dissensions are unfortunately visible and but few of their works are to be found now.

In 1629, D. de Fiesque, the agent of the duke of Lorraine divided in two the magnificent room of the Dormitory and under the pretext of increasing the light of the cells, sapped the interior splayings of the windows by cutting the small columns of the arches which adorn the walls.

Jacques de Souvré and the sir de la Chastière had obtained from Louis XIV the permission that the guard of the castle and its government should be intrusted to the Abbot The garrison consisted of only four or five soldiers. Louis XV took one part of the Abbey and confined prisoners in the dungeons; there were eighteen in 1776. In 1745, Victor de la Castagne, better known by the name of Dubourg, was shut up in the cage built, it is said, by Louis XI to imprison the famous cardinal La Balluc. This celebrated cage, called iron-cage, though it was of wood, was destroyed in 1777 by the comte d'Artois (Charles X) during his visit to Mont Saint-Michel.

In 1776 after a fire by lightning, the portal of the church was split and threatened ruin; four of the seven arcades of the nave were destroyed and the romanesque portal of Robert de Torigni had as a substitute a front in the style of that epoch ; called Jesuites style. In 1790 the monks were dispersed and the whole Abbey was transformed in to a prison in which the Revolution crammed three hundred priests of the dioceses of Avranches, Coutances and Rennes.

In 1811 Napoleon the First converted Mont Saint-Michel in a *house of correction*, and Louis XVIII made it a *central prison and house of correction*. Since those sad times, the works which have been done have only been of a particl and profane character.

The old Hostelry — built by Robert de Torigni — which had become a prison for women, collapsed in 1817 and threatened during a long time to drag with it the ruin of the south west part of the building. The magnificent halls of the Merveille were divided into floors in which were huddled the prisoners and their looms. The church itself suffered the most profane transformations; the chancel was alone spared and kept its altar, which saved this part of the church from the ravages of the fire in 1834, which wrought the greatest damages in the romanesque nave. This was the thirteenth fire since the foundation of the Abbey.

Restorations were undertaken from 1838 to 1850: three pillars in the south part were restored, but they have not the romanesque character of the other pillars of the nave which they tried to imitate. The other burnt parts were hidden from sight; the damages caused on the columns, walls and burnt arches have been concealed with plaster and recovered by a layer of mortar in *simili-granit*; cornices in peculiar styles have been made with the same stuff. These repairs are not sufficient, and are chiefly dangerous because these replasterings, dissembling the disorders which have taken place in these constructions will prevent people from seing the danger of their situation and therefore they will not remedy it in good time. The romanesque nave has been covered by a modern wood and plaster vault, the forms of which call to mind pretty nearly the works of the twelfth century; it is also in a very bad state.

A decree dated the 20th of october 1863 suppressed the prison and the Minister of the interior abandoned Mont Saint-Michel which became the property of an estate. In 1865 the Abbey with its dependencies, was let for nine years to the bishop of Coutances and Avranches, who ordered partitions and planks to be made dividing into work-shops the floors of the Merveille, the abbatial *Logis* and the church; he cleaned and drained the buildings and he ordered some repairs to be made with the annual help of 20000 francs which he obtained in 1865 to 1870 from Napoleon III.

In 1872, the minister of public instruction and fine arts ordered the state of Mont Saint-Michel to be looked into and ordered schemes of its restoration to be prepared (1). The report sent to the President of the Republic was approved of and by a decree of the 20th of april 1874 the estate of the Abbey of Mont Saint-Michel was declared an historical building so as to assure its conservation. From that time, the state took care not only of the great works, but assured their being kept in order as well as the local reparations of the buildings. They were let till 1886 to the monks of the order of Saint-Edme of Pontigny, established on Mont Saint-Michel since 1865. The buildings thus let are composed of the old abbatial Logis only with its dependences on the south.

From 1873, the minister of the public instruction and fine arts, through care of the commission of historical buildings has undertaken important works of consolidation and restoration (2). The object of these works has been : the

---

(1) According to his decision dated of the 14th of May 1872, the Minister of public instruction, of public worship and of fine arts gave us this charge. The studies of the actual condition (in 1872) and of the restoration belong to the Ministry and are placed in the archives of the Commission of historical buildings : they have been exhibited at the Salon of Paris in 1873, 1874 and 1875 and at the universal exhibition of 1878. — See the illustrations 4 and 5, south front in its state in 1872 and the same front supposed to be restored.

(2) The works are done under our authority and under the direction of M. Louvel, an architect, inspector of works of historical buildings, and by M. Fouché, contractor of public works.

construction of a strong buttress at the angle south west of the buildings in order to prevent their tumbling down : the underpinning of the pillars, walls and vaults of the romanesque substructures as well as those added on the west by Robert de Torigni in the twelfth century; the restoration of the flagging at the end of the eighteenth century, — after the suppressing of the first three arcades of the nave — and forming the ground of the large platform, on the west, before the actual front of the church. — The old flagging was buried under a bed of ground covered by a common layer which was saturated with water which infiltrated in the vaults and underground walls and thus caused great damages; — the underpinning of the basis of the ruined Hostelry the split walls of which would have caused the destruction of the southern place of the romanesque bases and adjacent buildings; the construction of a counterfort to strength the wall of the western front; the repairing of the chapel Saint-Etienne on the south and at last, what was the most important and interesting part of the undertaking works, *i. e.* the restoration of the Cloister, begun in 1877 and entirely finished in 1881. — See : Cloister. — The works were continued and include principally the restoration of the Dormitory, begun in 1882.

The fortified enclosure was an integral part of the outworks of the Abbey and of course belonged to it; however the town of Mont Saint-Michel had made the pretention of owning the altered ramparts in 1855, pretention which it renounced without any restriction by a deliberation dated of the 13th of october 1878, thanks to the initiative of its mayor M. Leplat, an intelligent and devoted administrator the recent lost of whom has been deeply felt by the inhabitants and by his numerous friends.

The restoration of the ramparts has been commenced; the Barbican before the gate of the town has been repaired; the *Avancée* of the Barbican and its postern have been cleared from the walls and the dung hole which embarrassed it. The english bombards — left by the Englishmen routed at the time of their last attack in 1434, — adorning the second door, but stopping the lateral postern have been placed on a platform which, though it does not take the place of the primitive tumbrels which they used as gun carriages, allows at least the examination in every detail of these curious species of the artillery of the fifteenth century.

The works would have certainly been cont'nued, if they had not been suddenly interrupted by an embankment erected near the ramparts, in spite of the greatest protests. This embankment, pompously but very improperly called a *dike* (for the word *dike* gives an idea of protection, and in this case this word is a synonyme of destruction), has had disastrous consequences. The tumbling down of a part of the small curtain of the rampart, which happened in january 1881, the crevices and the cracks of the towers of the king, of the *Escadre* and the curtains which join them, prove it too clearly and it would be childish to deny these destructive effets which are the consequence of a work as dangerous as it is of little use.

This work made with great effort offers this particularity that it was not asked for by any one, not even by these who were the most directly interested in its execution, *i. e.* by the Montois. For it has been now proved that not one of the inhabitants of the mount was in favour of or against the preparatory enquiry. We must notice, that by an act of authority absolutely arbitrary, the plan of the breakwater or to speak more exactly of the embankment was modified during its execution, without any new enquiry, and instead of its finishing at the rock on the left of the entrance, it rests against the walls which must give way (1). The undertaking cannot be explained; moreover it has always been without explanation; for we cannot consider as such a slow and only slightly disinterested petition or the recent and peculiar protestation, made by some inhabitants, with the form of deliberation, which contained *four signatures!!!* one of which was approximately a signature, an absurd and affected fact which Monsieur Prudhomme, the immortal model of ridiculous vanity and sufficiency, would not certainly disavow. It is impossible to take into account more seriously an anonymous petition presented by a *Bas-Normand to Messieurs les Députés*, a stupid work of distracted brains, the author of which, who is little indulgent for mental affections, about which he speaks much, in page 15 of is small treatise, is not sufficiently disguised by the deception which he has prudently assumed.

Public opinion which on this occasion could be more justly called public sense, has declared itself against this enterprise with as much strength as unanimity. The papers have boldly spoken about it from 1879, but without any result till now. However, we can believe that its endeavours, which are always generous and fair, will have

---

(1) We have exhibited this year at the Salon — Architecture — plans and drawings, made with the greatest care and exactness, showing the ramparts in 1879, what they are in 1883, and nothing at the same time the destructive effects of the embankment since 1879.

their fruit and that the courageous and legitimate claims of MMrs Lockroy and Jules Roche, brought before parliament in 1881 and 1882, will be at last listened to and will give again to Mont Saint-Michel its insular situation which will assure the preservation of its ramparts, which have endured for centuries.

The pressing works of restoration will then be recommenced with some purpose, and the commission of historical buildings, faithful to their traditions, will continue their labours by keeping intact an edifice, unique in France and which by the beauty of its buildings, its greatness, and the historical remembrances it recalls to our minds, presents the most beautiful specimens of the religious, monastic and military architecture of our dear fatherland.

Paris, April 3, 1883.

MONT SAINT-MICHEL

SOUTH FRONT

CONDITION IN 1872 AND PLAN OF RESTORATION

GENERAL VIEWS

Ed. Corroyer del.

Fig. 4. — General view of the South front. — Condition in 1872.

Ed. Corroyer del.   Fig. 5. — General view of the South front. — Plan of Restoration.

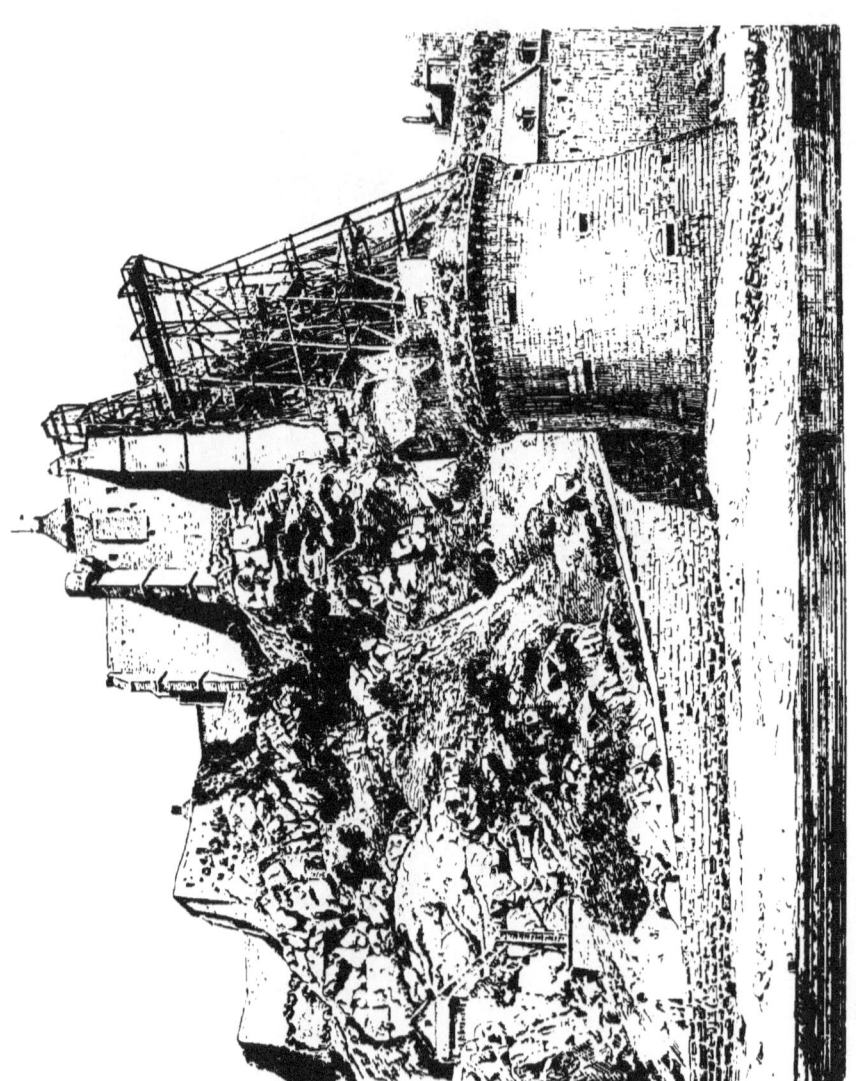

Fig. 6. — Scaffolding for the works of Restoration. — West front, 1878.

ITINERARY

The plans and numerous illustrations in the tex give an idea of the different edifices of Mont Saint-Michel; but it is useful to supplement them by explanations to facilitate the visit, often very quickly paid to the Abbey and its surroundings. At first it is necessary to know where you are, visitors generally forget to take this precaution which is necessary here to see thoroughly the many buildings of which Mont Saint-Michel is composed. The church can be used as a compass, if this expression may be employed, for its large longitudinal axis extends from east to west and of course its transverse axis and its transepts go from north to south.

Therefore we counsel the visitors to go first to the church; we will refer to this again later on, but we think that before examining details it is better to see the general appearance of Mont Saint-Michel, which we suppose to be without the embankment which encumbers it on the south.

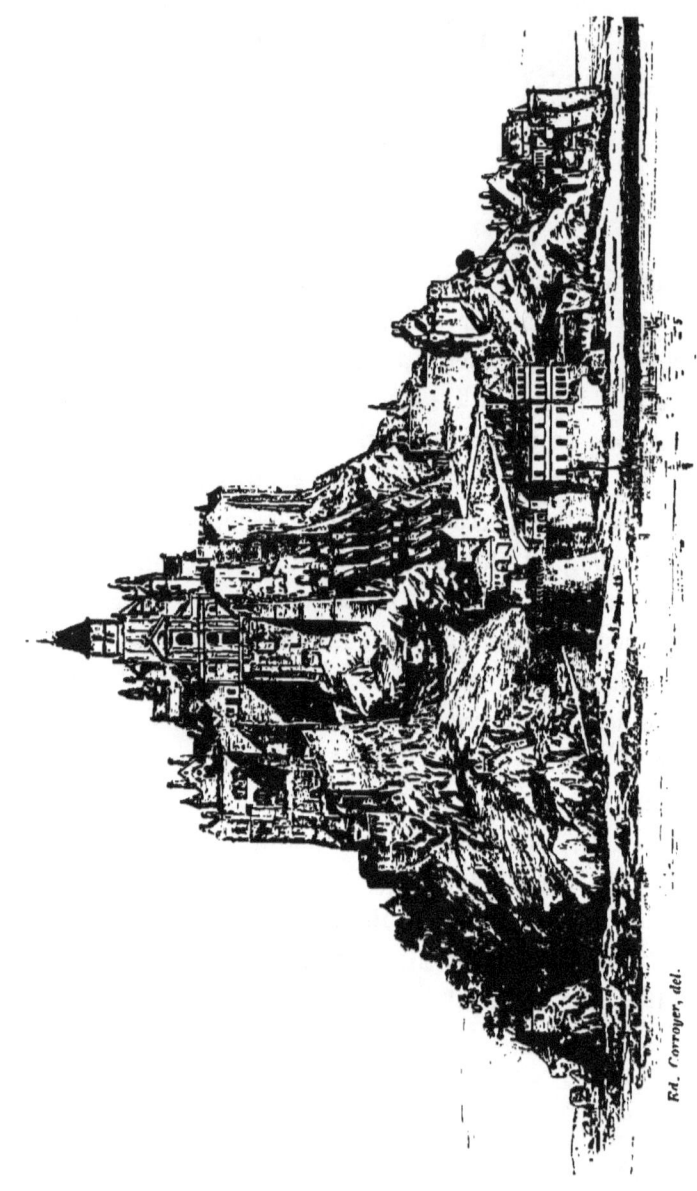

Ed. Corroyer, del.

Fig. 7. — General view of the West front. — Condition in 1872.

GENERAL VIEW

The approach to the Mount is easier at the time of the neap tides, corresponding, as every one knows, with the first and last quarter of the moon, because you can drive there independent of the tide, for the sea does not then surround the Mount or, in any case, does not prevent crossing the shingle. You can see, on arrival, the south front of Mont Saint-Michel — fig. 4 — and you can always, when the sea is low, walk round it. You must then go near the rock or the ramparts and the sight of the Abbey is necessarily shortened, and entirely changed, for being so near its most beautiful aspects are deformed. Always at low water, but principally at neaptide, you can advance on the shingle on the east, and see one of the most beautiful views of the Mount and its whole development; but the west and north coasts are not so easy to be reached by the same means, because you must cross the river on the west, and the shoals on the north, which it is not prudent to do without a guide, these expeditions not being always practicable on account of the sands more or less moving according to the tides which change and shift the ground.

Fig. 8. — General view of the North front. — Condition in 1872.

We think it is better to choose the occasion of the spring tides, especially when there is full moon, which permit us to go round the Mount in a boat; visitors easily find small vessels manned by fishermen of the Mount, who are courageous, experienced sailors and the safest guides that can be found. By embarking at the gate of the town, this voyage of circumnavigation may be made in less than an hour; it is the best means of seeing all the beauty of the Mount. The sight changes at every movement of the oars, if we can use this expression, and all the fronts of the old monastary seem to be unrolled, offering successively the most imposing and most majestic aspects, especially on the west, on the north, on the northeast and on the east; it is a magnificent succession of views as picturesque as can be imagined, and nothing can better help the study of the exterior architecture of the different edifices of the Mount.

A trip made at the time of the spring tides we have just spoken about, offers other advantages which will be especially appreciated by artists : chiefly the advantage of seeing Mont Saint-Michel, its Abbey, its ramparts and its shingles surrounded and covered with the sea, brilliantly lighted by the moon and offering, particularly during the beautiful summer nights, the most fantastic and the most unexpected effects. But what is invaluable is the incomparable view which can be

Fig. 9. — General view of the East front. — Plan of restoration.

Ed. Corroyer, del.

seen either from the ramparts on the east and on the north, or still better from the large upper platform on the west, and which the shingles of Mont Saint-Michel offer alone, *i. e.* the " *arrival* " of the sea. We use on purpose this expression : the *arrival of the sea*, because it suits alone this occasion.

The sea having withdrawn more than 12 kilometres from the Mount when it is low water, *arrives* at the moment of the surge, announcing itself by a roaring at first confused and which soon becomes a frightful noise and forms a formidable bar, an eddy of water, in the rivers which flow on the shores and on the whole extent of the vast estuary which it soon covers entirely. This immense sheet of water overflowing the shores not with the rapidity of a horse going full gallop, as it has been hyperbolically said, but going forward by a continuel movement, with an implacable strength, produces an extraordinary effect.

If the phenomena of the tides are always so interesting to be studied and so curious to be seen, they are especially surprising on the shores of Mont Saint-Michel, where they are manifested, principally at the time of the equinoxes under special conditions and present majestic views which leave on our mind the liveliest impressions.

When the wind forces the tide, the waters leap over the first two gates of the town and bathe the English

Fig. 10. — King's gate, XVth century.
(View taken from the gate of the Barbican, 2nd gate.

bombards, trophies of the assault of 1434, which adorn the *Avancée* of the town.

The sea falls almost as quickly as it rises; an hour after the retiring of the tide, you can go out of the town, and a very little time afterwards, walk round the rock and the ramparts.

When you have seen the general view of Mont Saint-Michel under its exterior aspects, and finished your trip round the island which you began on the south west, you land on the south on the narrow rocky shingle or on the ground which is in front of the *Avancée* and after crossing it as well as the Barbican forming the exterior defences, you arrive at the King's gate which leads you to the town, the only street of which conducts you to the Abbey.

We will speak about these interesting buildings on coming back, and supposing that the reader continues to follow us, we will ascend the street of the town while giving him some details about its origin, in order to reach quickly the top of the rock and the church which is going to be the point of separation for the methodical visit to the Abbey and its dependencies.

THE TOWN

The origin of the village or rather, according to tradition, of the town of Mont Saint-Michel, is very old, if we believe the chroniclers, who tell us it was in the tenth century, as we have seen in the historical notice. The small borough had the same destiny as the Monastery at the foot of which its houses were grouped on escarpments of rock on the east, which formed a natural defence against the encroachments of the sea and attacks of men. It increased continually strengthened on its weak parts by palisades and at the time of the rebuilding of the Edifices of the Abbey, from the thirteenth to the fourteenth century, it was likewise surrounded by strong walls forming the first fortified enclosure of the Monastery.

The town enlarged in the fifteenth century and surrounded, from 1415 to 1420, by a wall extending more on the east and on the south than elsewhere, has only one entrance opening to the south, on the west side of its ramparts, the gate of which is preceded by works covering its approaches. After passing through the narrow passages of the *Avancée* and of the *Barbican*, we reach the principal gate, the King's gate, which leads us to the town.

Fig. 11. — Street of the Town.

The only street of the town has on each side houses some of which are still as they probably were in the middle ages. They do not offer any thing very curious in their details; however, by their union and their arrangement, they form a picturesque whole of which figure 11 gives an idea.

There still exists in the high part of the town some traces of the primitive constructions retaining romanesque forms of the twelfth and thirteenth century; they are the remnants of the old town built on the most elevated part of the rock on the east of the Abbey or, according to some historians, the ruins of a convent for women, restored, it is said by Duguesclin, and near which he wished a *Beau Logis* to be built which his wife Tiphaine de Raguenel inhabited from 1366 to 1374, during her sojourn at Mont Saint-Michel. The houses of the lower part of the town and those of the southern water-shed, were not built at a later date than the fifteenth century. The country church, built about 1440, has nothing remarkable but a tomb-stone of older date than its foundation.

The town has always been inhabited by fishermen: but the greatest part of the dwellings of the old town and of the new one have always been as they are now, hostelries for pilgrims or shops where were sold the pictures or *enseignes du benoist Arcange Monsieur Saint-Michel*, and where every kind of objects of piety are still

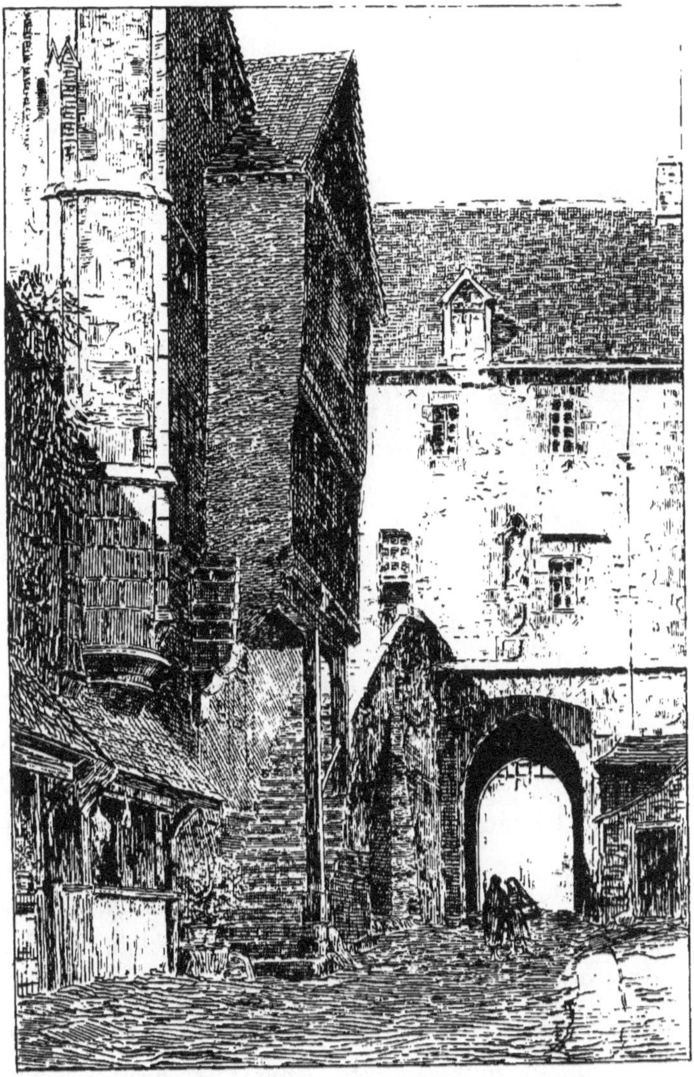

Ed. Corroyer, del.

Fig. 12. — Interior of the Town. — King's gate and watch tower.
(View taken from the *Hôtel Saint-Michel.*)

sold. The archæologists give us curious information about several of the old hostelries, among them, the inn which is before the watch tower; this was the *Tête d'or*, very fashionable in the seventeenth century. It

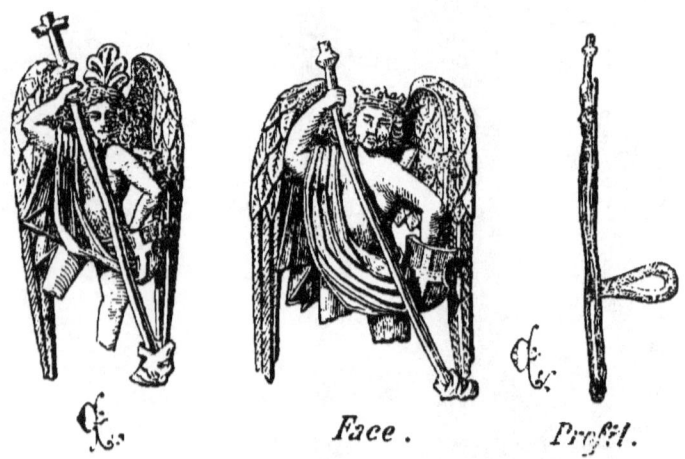

Fig. 13 et 14. — Representations or *enseignes* of Saint-Michel, Stamps of pilgrimage found in the Seine in Paris.

was called successively Hotel of the *Tête d'or* and of *Saint-Michel*, and became afterwards the *hotel Poulard*, keeping however its reputation, for it is still the best hostelry in the town.

The shops and the sellers of images or of *quencaillerie* were always very numerous at Mont Saint-Michel. We have collected a great number of specimens of *stamps of pilgrimage* in which there was a considerable traffic in the middle ages. A part of these *enseignes*

MONT SAINT-MICHEL

Fig. 15. — Indented mould of a stamp of pilgrimage, XVth century (belonging to M. Ramé).

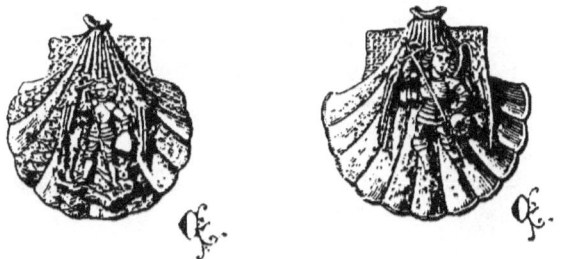

Fig. 16. — Moulds of Saint-Michel (XVth century).

were made in Paris, and the great quantity of them found in the bed of the Seine near the bridges reserved for the goldmiths, proves it absolutely.

There was also the manufacture of *stamps of pilgri-*

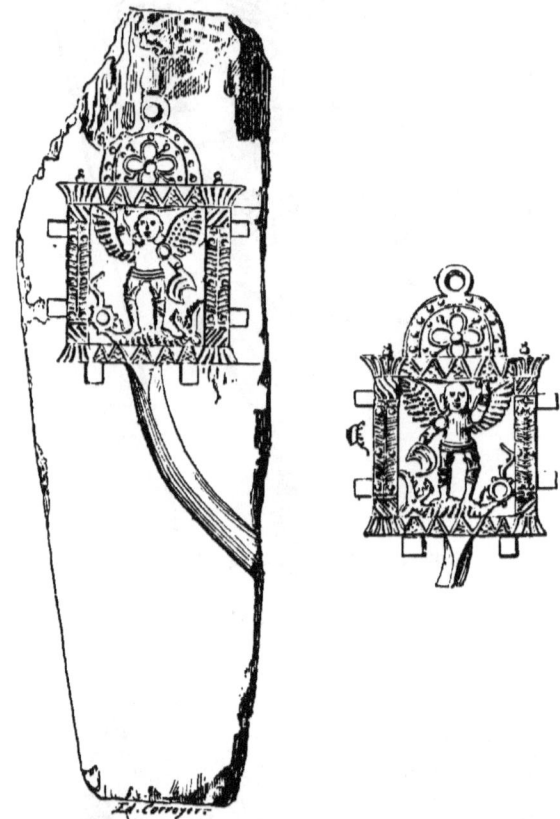

Fig. 17 et 18. — Indented mould and proof in relief of a stamp of pilgrimage found at Mont Saint-Michel.

mage at Mont Saint-Michel, as proved by the *enseigne* — fig. 3 — and the slate mould — fig. 17-18 — found in the search lately made by digging in the neighbourhood of the Abbey.

The street of the small town follows very nearly the line of the walls, and is on a level with the entrance till it reaches the tower, named Liberty's tower, it then rises quickly, winds about on the north on the slopes of the rock and ends by large flights of steps on the east, at the place where formerly rose the first gate of the *Grand Degré* leading to the Barbican from the Châtelet. Some very narrow lanes ascending the rock lead to the gardens in terraces or to the highest houses and end by turning to the exterior walls and to the Postern of the south staircase of the Barbican of the Châtelet protecting the entrance of the Abbey.

Ed. Corroyer, del.

Fig. 19. — The Châtelet. — Entrance of the Abbey.

THE ABBEY

The church or Basilica has always been the centre and, as it were, the heart of the Abbey. It is the oldest construction of the Mount; the different buildings and the town itself have been successively grouped around it : and they make a majestic basis for the old sanctuary of Saint-Michel and form by their assemblage a magnificent whole as wonderful by its picturesque situation as by the boldness of its conception and the great beauty of its details.

It seemed to us necessary to begin the visit by the church, in order to be able to describe clearly the edifices of different epochs, which are placed one over the other and to lead our reader in the turnings of so complicated a labyrinth.

Although this manner of proceeding is not inconformity with the details of the description of the topography of the Mount, yet it has seemed to us the most rational and the most useful, because it will allow us to follow the construction of the Basilica, of the buildings of the Abbey and of the Ramparts.

The following plans — fig. 20, 21 and 22 — seem to us absolutely necessary, as well as the sections — fig. 24 and 25. These drawings, by giving the right idea of

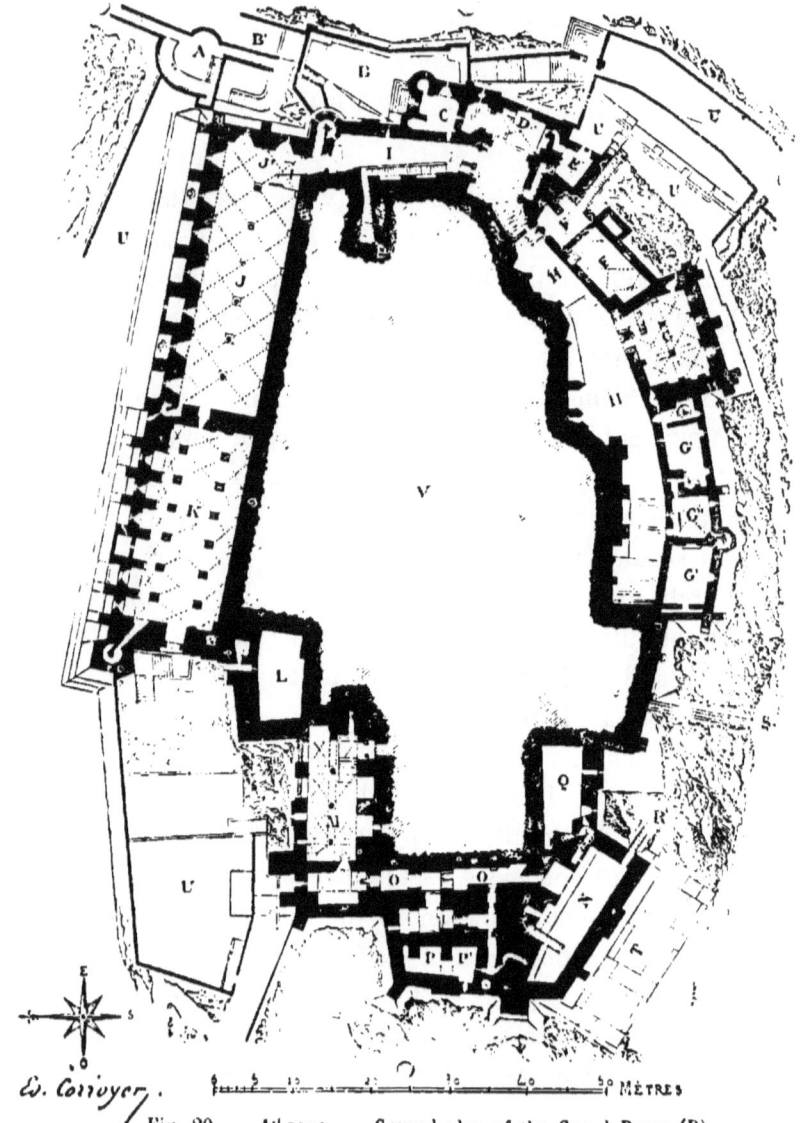

Fig. 20. — 1st zone. — Ground plan of the Guard Room (D), of the Almonry (J) and of the Cellar (K).

the buildings placed one over the other, of their grouping and of their forms, at different levels, will help to guide the visitors without confusion in the maze of their innumerable divisions.

EXPLANOTORY NOTE
Fig. 20.

A	Claudine tower. — Ramparts.
B	First fortified enclosure, or Barbican, surrounding the Châtelet and protecting the entrance to the Abbey.
B'	Ruins of the large flight of steps.
C	Châtelet. — Lower part, staircase overlooked by the Châtelet and leading to the Guard Room.
D	Guard Room (Belle-Chaise).
E	Perrine tower.
F	Proxy's office and Baillif's office of the Abbey.
G	Abbatial dwelling.
G'	Lodgings of the Abbey.
G"	Sainte-Catharine's chapel.
H	Church yard and staircase leading to the higher church.
I	Court of the Merveille, — between Belle-Chaise and the Merveille.
J	Almonry Room ⎫
J'	Ruins of a furnace ⎬ Merveille.
K	Cellar ⎭
L	Old abbatial dwellings. — Kitchens — (End of the XIth century).
M	Gallery or Crypt of the *Aquilon* (Roger II).
N	Basement of the Hostelry (Robert de Torigni).
O	Passages communicating with the Hostelry.
P and P'	Prisons (Under P' cells called Twins' cells).
Q	Bases of Saint-Stephen's chapel.
R	Ruin of the old *poulain* (Robert de Torigni).
S	Modern *poulain*.
T	Wall supports, built in 1862 or 1863.
U	Gardens, terraces and narrow path round them.
V	Solid rock.

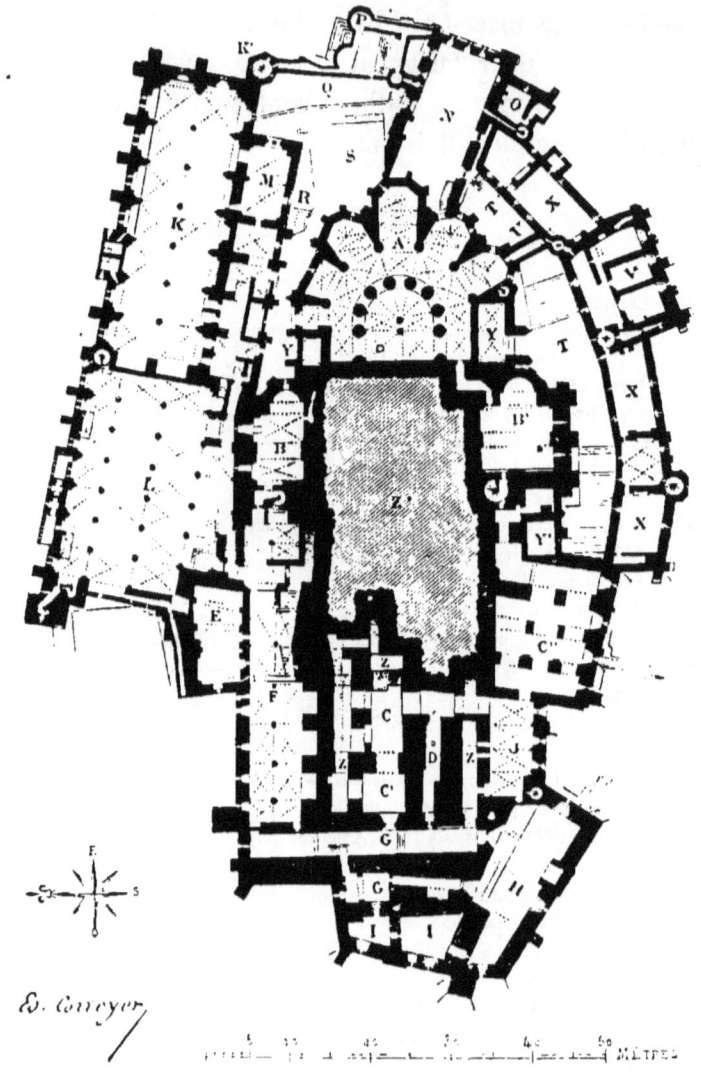

Fig. 21. — 2nd zone. Ground plan of the lower church (A), of the Refectory (K) and of the knights' hall (L).

EXPLANATORY NOTE
Fig. 21.

A   Lower church or crypt, called the great pillars.
B   Chapel under the north transept.
B'   Chapel under the south transept (Saint-Martin).
C   Basement of the romanesque nave.
C' and C   Charnel-house or Cemetery of the monks.
C"   Romanesque under-basements (under the platform called Saut-Gaultier)
D   Old cistern.
E   Old abbatial buildings. — (Refectory). — End of the XIth century.
F   Old cloister or walking-place (Roger II).
G   Passages communicating with the Hostelry.
H   Hostelry.   } Robert de Torigni.
I   Out buildings of the Hostelry. }
J   Saint Stephen's chapel.
K   Refectory.
K'   Tower of the Corbins.   } Merveille.
L   Knights' hall.
M   Chapel.
N   Hall of the Officers and of the Government. — Belle-Chaise.
O   Perrine tower.
P   Battlements of the Châtelet.
Q   Court yard of the Merveille.
R   Staircase leading from the court of the Merveille to the terrace S.
S   Terrace of the Apse.
T   Court yard of the church.
U   Fortified bridge joining the lower church to the abbatial dwelling.
V   Abbatial dwelling.
X   Lodgings of the Abbey.
Y   Cisterns (XVth century).
Y'   Cisterns (XVIth century).
Z   Staircase leading from the underground to the higher church.
Z'   Solid rock.

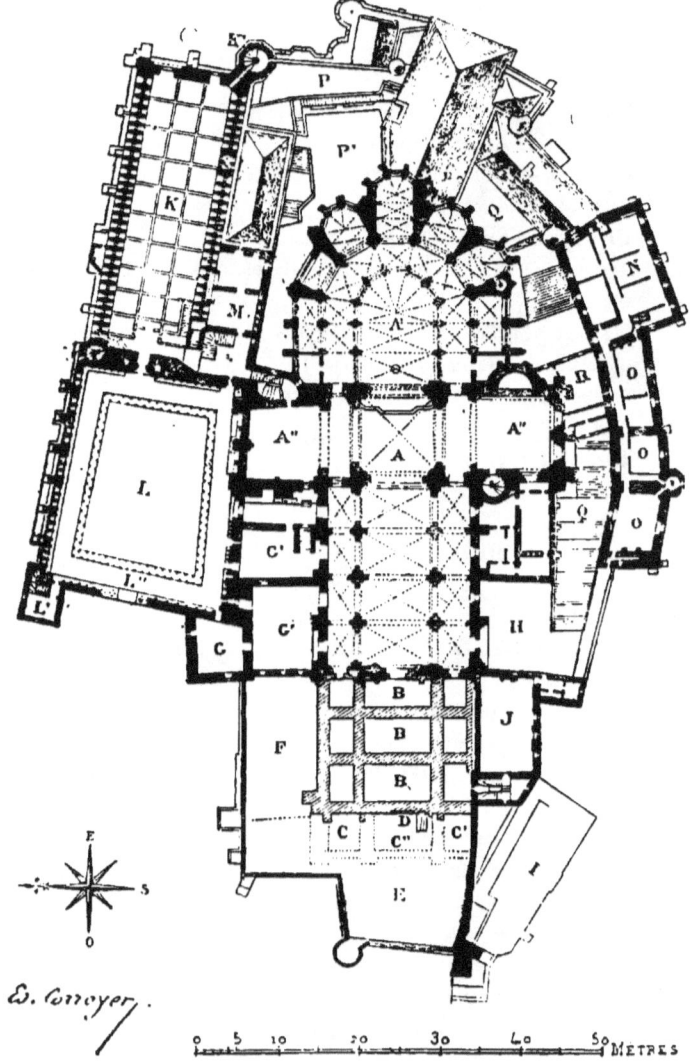

Fig. 22. — 3rd zone. Ground plan of the higher church (A), of the Cloister (L) and of the Dormitory (K).

MONT SAINT-MICHEL

EXPLANATORY NOTE

Fig. 22.

	A	Higher church.
	A'	Chancel.
	A"	North and south transepts.
Remnants found in 1875 under the flagging of the large platform.	B.B.B	The first three triforiums of the romanesque nave (destroyed in 1776).
	C and C'	Towers in front of the romanesque portal. } Robert
	C"	Porch between the two towers. } de Torigni.
	D	Grave of Robert de Torigni and of D. Martin de Furmendeio (?)
	E	Old court in the front of the church.
	F	Site of the hall called of Souvré (hall of the Chapter; old dormitory).

G   Old abbatial buildings (Dormitory: end of the XIth century).
G' Actual sacristy (old dormitory).
H   Platform of the Saut-Gaultier (lateral entrance, south of the church).
I   Ruins of the Hostelry (Robert de Torigni).
J   Infirmaries.
K   Dormitory. (The separations have been made by the directors of the prison).
K' The Corbius.
L   Cloister.
L' Charters room.
L" Entrance of Chapter hall (designed and commenced in the XIIIth century).
M   Actual library (part of the old abbatial buildings, XIVth century).
N   Abbatial dwelling.
O   Lodgings of the Abbey.
P   Court of the Merveille.
P' Terrace of the Apse.
P   Court yard of the church and staircase leading to the Saut-Gaultier.
R   Kitchens (actual) of the monks, established on the wooden bridge (XVIth century).

GUARD ROOM — BELLE-CHAISE

After penetrating into the Barbican which protects the first gate and entering the Abbey — fig. 19 — by the fortified staircase under the Châtelet — an important point which we shall describe later on — we come to the Guard Room, at the level of which the plan of the first zone has been drawn fig. 20. This Guard Room is a part of the building called Belle-Chaise, erected by Richard Tustin, about 1250; at that time, the entrance to the Abbey was on the north side of this building on which opens a magnificent door which must be examined before passing through. It was closed by two panels, one of which was interior and the other exterior; on the lateral piers of this one you can still see the iron collars surrounding the posts with which the leaves were turned, externally. It was in this Guard Room that all comers deposited their arms before entering the monastery buildings, unless exempted by special permission of the Prior of the Abbey. In the first years of the XVth century Pierre le Roy opened a door and a postern in the north front giving on the court yard of the Merveille, a new entrance to the building which he commenced by joining the Merveille to the Châtelet; he built also the large chimney which stands opposite to the entrance door.

The Guard Room is vaulted and its architecture, simple and severe is suited to its objects. It is lighted on the east by a window surmounted by an *oculus;* in the second triforium on the south a small door opens on a staircase, built in the thickness of the wall, which leads to one of the floors of the Perrine tower, to the door keepers' room and by a detour to the large hall above. In the third triforium on the south is the oblique passage leading by a flight of steps to the court yard of the church — see plan fig. 20.

ABBATIAL BUILDINGS

The court yard of the church is formed : on the right by the beautiful *bases* of the chancel rebuilt in the second half of the XVth century by Guillaume d'Estouteville, and by the walls of the transept of the romanesque church and of the more recent constructions; on the left by the abbatial buildings, begun by Richard Tustin about 1250. They were continued, in the XIVth century by Nicolas le Vitrier and Geoffroy de Servon.

The lodgings of the Abbey then extended on the south of the church up to the west front of the south transept and were composed of several buildings one of which especially, the abbatial dwelling has a grand aspect. Pierre le Roy finished them about the end of the XIVth century.

Fig. 23. — Fortified bridge in the court yard of the church. (Restoration.)

At the north west angle of the abbatial dwelling, towards the court yard of the church, are to be seen the remnants of the arch of a bridge; this bridge joined the dwelling to the lower chapels of the chancel of the romanesque church; it was ruined at the same time as the romanesque chancel, in 1421.

A new bridge, the embattled parapet of which is sustained by machicolations with rich mouldings, was built lower down in the same court by the cardinal d'Estouteville at the same time as the new chancel commenced in 1450. This open passage, on the level of the chapels of the lower church and of one of the floors of the abbatial dwelling, affords a passage, through the lower chuch, between the Buildings on the south and those of the Merveille on the North; the plan of the second zone has been drawn at this level — fig. 21. — We give a perspective view of the fortified bridge, taken from the south door of the Guard Room — fig. 23.

In the first years of the XVIth century, Guillaume de Lamps, an abbot of the Mount gave orders for the erection of the building joining the south transept and running parallel with the south side of the nave. He pulled down the flights of steps leading from the Guard Room to the church and he ordered the large flight of steps to be made which still exists as well as the platform called the Saut-Gaultier, which terminates it and on which opens the south Portal of the church. This abbot ordered also a wooden bridge to be erected, now worm-eaten, which joins the higher church to the abbatial buildings.

The construction of the building, joining the south collateral of the church and the transept, as well as the construction of the large flight of steps have greatly modified this part of the Abbey. Until the end of the XVth century the staircase led from the court yard of the church to the south lateral door. It established the necessary communications between the higher church and the west substructions where stood the Charnel-house or cemetery of the monks and in front of which was the mortuary chapel, so called of the *thirty wax-tapers*. — This was under the Saut-Gaultier, where now may be seen the large wheel — the entrance to it was on the east, at the foot of the south side-aisle. Some traces ofe the old arrangement, before the building of the large actual staircase, still exist in some parts of the underground vaults on the south.

From the beginning of the XVIth century to our time, and after the fires of 1564 and 1594 which caused so much damage, the lodgings of the Abbey underwent important changes especially as regards their roofs : the extent of which may be judged by a comparison of figures 4 and 5.

THE CHURCH

After ascending the large staircase leading to the platform of Saut-Gaultier and admiring the beautiful sight which you see from this eminence, you walk in the Basilica by the lateral Portal opened in the south collateral of the romanesque church.

Before visiting the higher church, you must first look at the large west platform from which you can perceive the sea making the horizon a splendid panorama, and the considerable substructures which are the bases of the church and of the north, west and south buildings, and which give an idea of the great difficulties which the first builders had to surmount to realize their monumental conceptions.

As we have seen in the historical notice, the church was begun in 1020 by Hildebert II, sixth regular abbot of the Mount from 1017 to 1023, whom Richard II entrusted with the details of the works. We must attribute to this abbot the substructures of the romanesque church which, especially on the west side have gigantic proportions. This part of the Mount is one of the most interesting to be studied; it shows the greatness and the audacity of the work of the architect Hildebert. Instead of cutting into the top of the mountain and

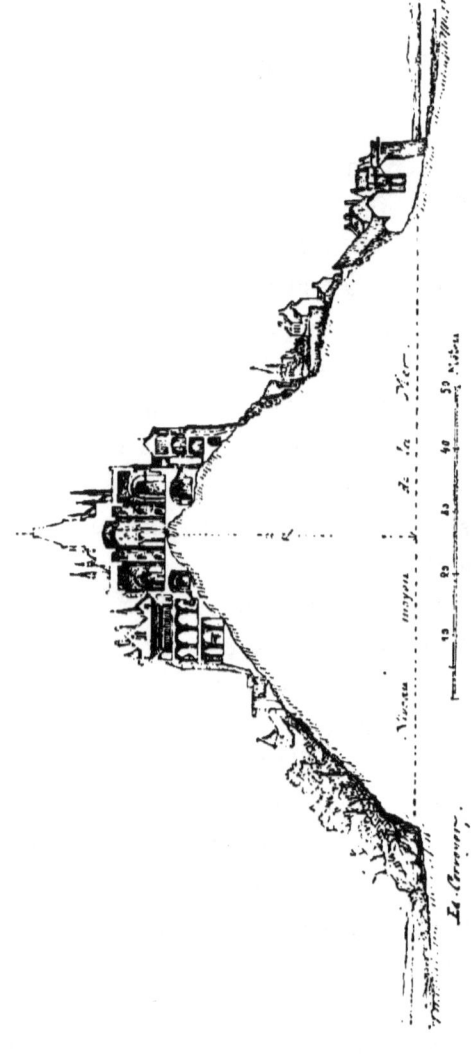

Fig. 24. — Transversal section of Mont Saint-Michel (from the north to the south).

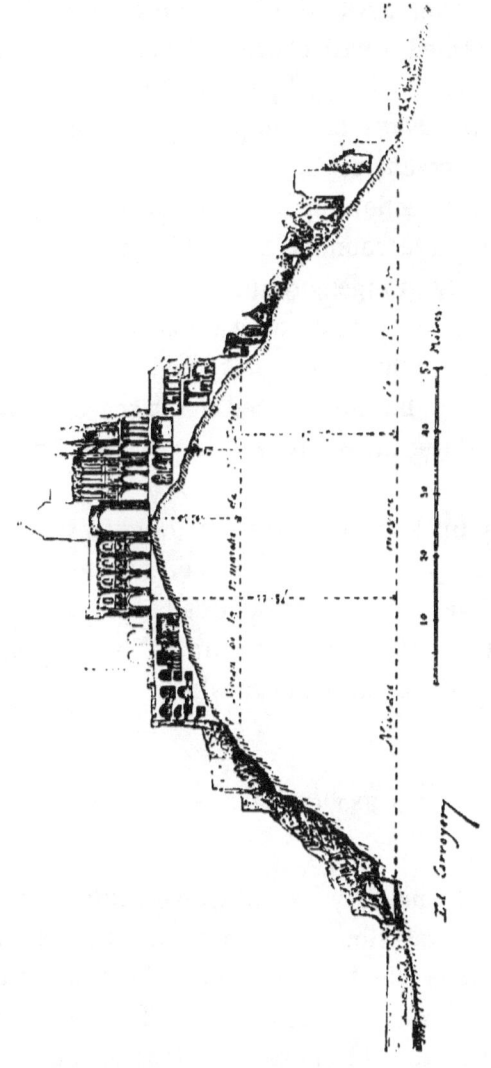

Fig. 25. — Longitudinal section of Mont Saint-Michel (from the west to the east).

principally in order not to diminish the majesty of the pedestal, he formed a vast plateau, the centre of which is on the level of the highest part of the rock and the sides rest on the walls and on piers joined by vaults and make a basement of perfect firmness.

The transverse section (fig. 24) shows the romanesque constructions surrounded by buildings which have been successively grouped around it at different times. It shows on the north and south transepts, the crypts or lower chapels, which have not been cut in the roc, as it has been said, but constructed in the space between the declivity of the mountain and the plateau built by Hildebert.

The longitudinal section, figure 25, shows the basements of the west already referred, to and those of the east. The romanesque substructures have disappeared covered by those of the XVth century at the time of the construction of the enlarged chancel.

SUBSTRUCTURES

On leaving the nave by a small gate on the north and descending several steps, we arrive at the primitive abbatial buildings which, at the end of the XIth century, extended to the north of the church. The visitor will see in succession the old Cloister or place to walk in for the monks, built by Roger II, in the early part of the XIIth century, and at the west end, one of the floors of

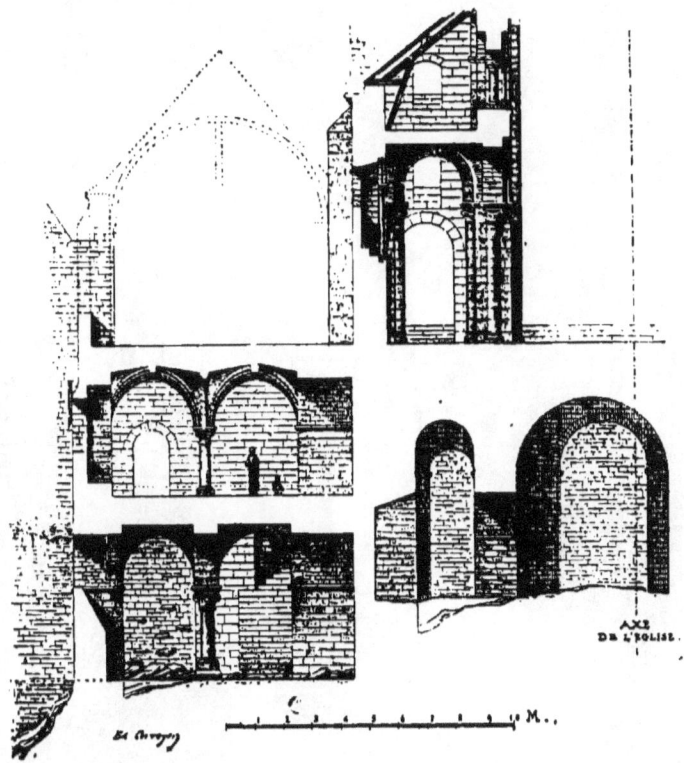

Fig. 26. — Edifice of Roger II, on the north of the nave.
(Section from the north to the south).

the constructions of Robert de Torigni; afterwards by going down and stopping half-way he will observe the old charnel-house or cemetery of the monks; also Saint-

Ed. Corroyer, del.

Fig. 27. — Gallery of the *Aquilon* (XIIth century).

Stephen's chapel now communicating by an opening with the old chapel of the Thirty wax-tapers — under the Saut-Gaultier — where is placed the great wheel used to draw up the stores. Afterwards, on descending the staircase, which he has left, he reaches the gallery of the *Aquilon*, — lower cloister — he will further descend to see the subterranean floors, the prisons and the dungeons of the Abbey, the ruins of the Hostelry, as well as the edifices on the west in front of the romanesque constructions built by Robert de Torigni. This part of the Abbey is very curious. Fig. 28 shows the

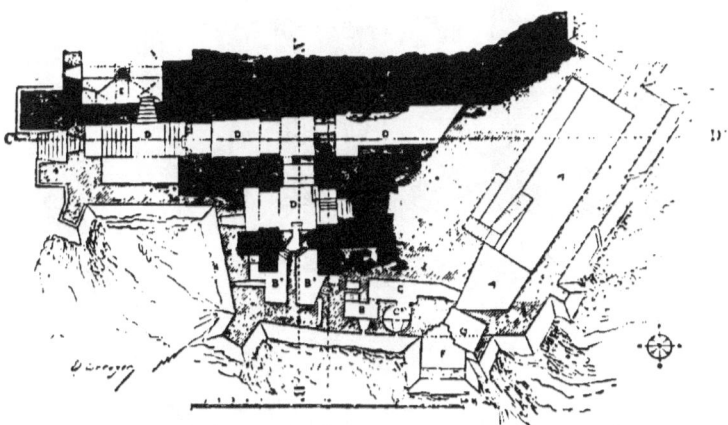

Fig. 28. — Constructions of Robert de Torigni. — Plan of the basements.

plans of the basements — the black tints indicate the romanesque parts and the *grey marks* the Edifices of Robert de Torigni. — A is the cellar of the Hostelry, where you see on the east, A, the *toothing* of the declivity of the rock reaching to the warehouses of the Abbey; B' and B' the dungeons named the *Twins;* C a passage leading from the Hostelry to the cell B and to the staircase C'; C' the staircase leading to the above prison; D the passages communicating with the dun-

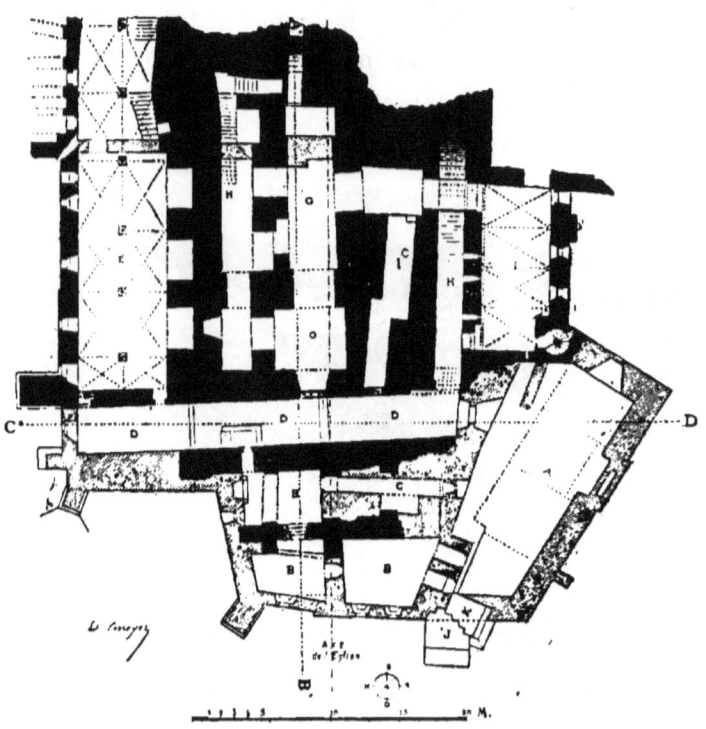

Fig. 29. — Constructions of Robert de Torigni.
Ground plan of the ambulatory.

geons, with the prisons above, and on nearly the same level, with the gallery of the *Aquilon* E; E the buttress built in 1618 and G that which was built in 1873.

The plan, fig. 29, gives the details of the same constructions above and at a level with the old Cloister or ambulatory. A is the infirmary; B, its dependencies; C, the passage joining the offices; D, the communication between the infirmary and the regular buildings of the Abbey; E, the Cloister; F, Saint-Stephen's chapel (XIIIth century); G, the charnel-house or cemetery of the monks; H,, the staircase leading to the higher church; I, the cistern; J, the buttress of 1618 and K that of 1873.

The figure 30 shows the tranverse section of the romanesque constructions; parts obliquely stippled indicate the constructions added by Robert de Torigni; in A stands the grave of this celebrated Abbot; and in B that of his successor Don Martin; they were both found in 1875 under the large west platform, at the basis of the towers built from 1180 to 1185 in front of the romanesque portal.

At last by again ascending the staircases by which we went down, we shall be again in the romanesque church which was, as we have already stated, begun in 1020 and finished in 1135 by Bernard du Bec, XIIIth Abbot of the Mount from 1131 to 1149.

Fig. 30. — Constructions of Robert de Torigni.
(Transverse section, from the north to the south, running parallel with the line CD of the plans).

This immense building, erected in honour of Saint-Michel and of his ancient worship, on the artificial plateau built or commenced by Hildebert, had the form of a latin cross, represented by the *Nave* composed of seven arcades, by the two *transepts* and lastly by the *chancel*. Of the romanesque church there still exist: four arcades of the nave; the pillars and the triumphal arches which sustained the romanesque steeple, or at least that which Bernard du Bec erected in the first half of the XIIth century; the two transepts, the two semi-circular chapels built in the fronts of the transepts, and lastly the *toothings* of the chancel ruined in 1421.

THE NAVE

The nave of the church consisted, as we have already said, of seven arcades, the first three of which were destroyed in 1776. After its alteration, the nave was closed by a façade built in the fashion of that time, in the style called the *jésuits' style*, the peculiar architecture of which makes us regret the suppression of the nave and of the old portal. In front of the old portal was a court built on the romanesque substructures.

The work of restoration, commenced in 1873 under the direction of the commission of historical buildings, necessitated, in 1875, excavations under the flag-stones of the large platform of the west, which revealed the foundations of the first three arcades. The plan — fig. 31 — shows these discoveries; it indicates also: the constructions made in front of the romanesque portal by Robert de Torigni, this abbot's grave and his successor Don Martin's.

These traces have been covered over — after the useful works of preservation — by the flag-stones making the ground of the large plateau.

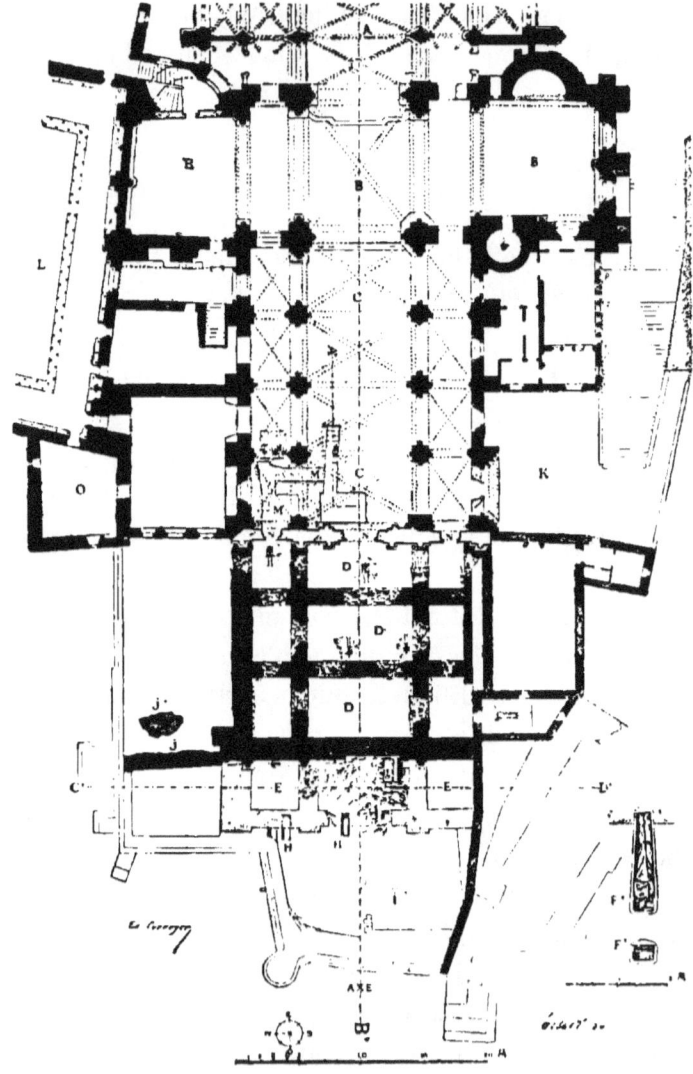

Fig. 31. — Plan of the church. — Actual nave. — Discoveries made in 1875.

EXPLANATORY NOTE

- A   Chancel (rebuilt in the XVth century).
- B   Transepts.   } Romanesque constructions
- C   Nave.   } XIth century.
- D   Foundations of the three destroyed arcades.
- E   Foundations of the towers and of the porch, built by Robert de Torigni (XIth century).
- F   Grave of Robert de Torigni.
- F'   Details of the grave of Robert de Torigni. } XIIth century.
- G   Grave of Don Martin de Furmedeio.
- H   Empty graves (XIth century.
- I   Traces of the flag-stones of the old court in front of the church.
- J   Ruins of the room called de Souvré's Room (old Dormitory).
- J'   Traces of the flag-stones of de Souvré's Room.
- K   Platform, called Saut-Gaultier.
- L   Cloister (XIIIth century).
- M   Ruins of the staircases leading down to the charnel-house of the Monks (XIth century).
- N   Front rebuilt in 1780.
- O   Old abbatial buildings (end of the XIth century).

The front nave of the church is formed of three parts, *i. e.* a large nave and two collaterals, rather narrow. Like most of the churches built at the beginning of the XIth century, especially in Normandy, the central nave was covered by visible timber-work. The actual vault which seems to be in stone, is really in wood and old dry plaster; it was made after the fire of 1834. The aisles are alone vaulted by projecting, lateral and transverse arches, the intervening spaces of which are full of plain groined vaults. The square piers are cantoned with engaged columns at the third of their diameter, as shown in the plan, fig. 32.

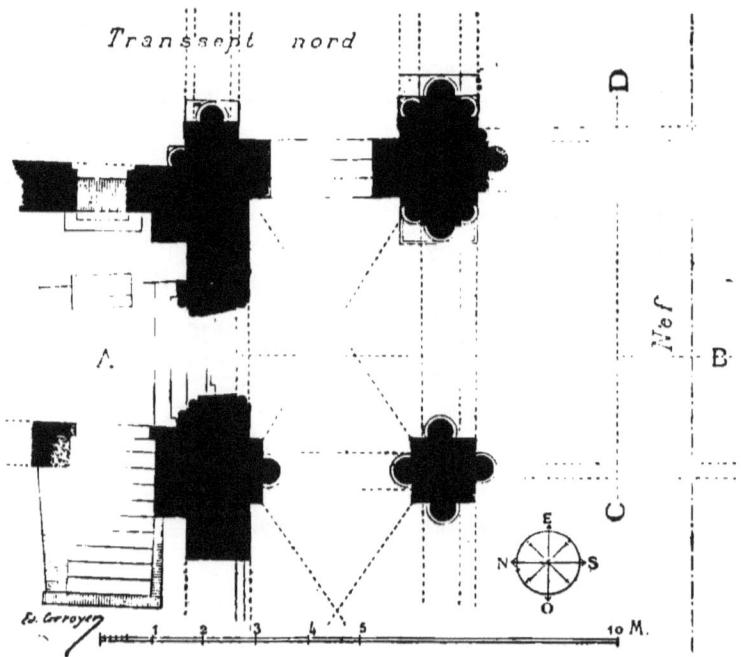

Fig. 32. — Plan of an arcade of the romanesque nave.

The columns at the side of the large nave, rise to the higher cornice : ended by the capitals, they supported the outside timber trusses. The other three columns crowned by capitals, support the transverse arches of the lateral wall and those of the aisles which longitudinally join the piers together and transversally these to the exterior walls. The figures 33 and 34 give the transversal and longitudinal section of an arcade of the nave, following the lines AB and CD of the plan fig. 32. The dotted lines show the form of the modern *pseudo-vault*.

The excavations made in 1875 at the actual entrance of the nave, have disclosed in the north aisle — M of the plan fig. 31 — the passages and the ruins of the staircase leading from the nave to the charnel-house or cemetery of the monks. A passage and a staircase both stand on the south, running parallel with Saint-Stephen's chapel — in J and in Z of the plan fig. 21. These communications were intercepted by the construction of the front in 1780.

At the intersection of the nave and the transepts stand the triumphal pillars erected in 1058, which supported the steeple, rebuilt several times but entirely destroyed at the end of the XVIth century. In its place the massive square pavilion was unhappily built in 1620 which still exists and which is proportionally too large for the four pillars; of these, two remain almost perpendicular as well as the transverse arches which join them; but the two pillars joining the chancel suffered much damage from the fire of 1421. They are injured and split, and it was impossible to support them but by building the chancel in the XVth century, the arches of the first arcade of which have been put to support them. The

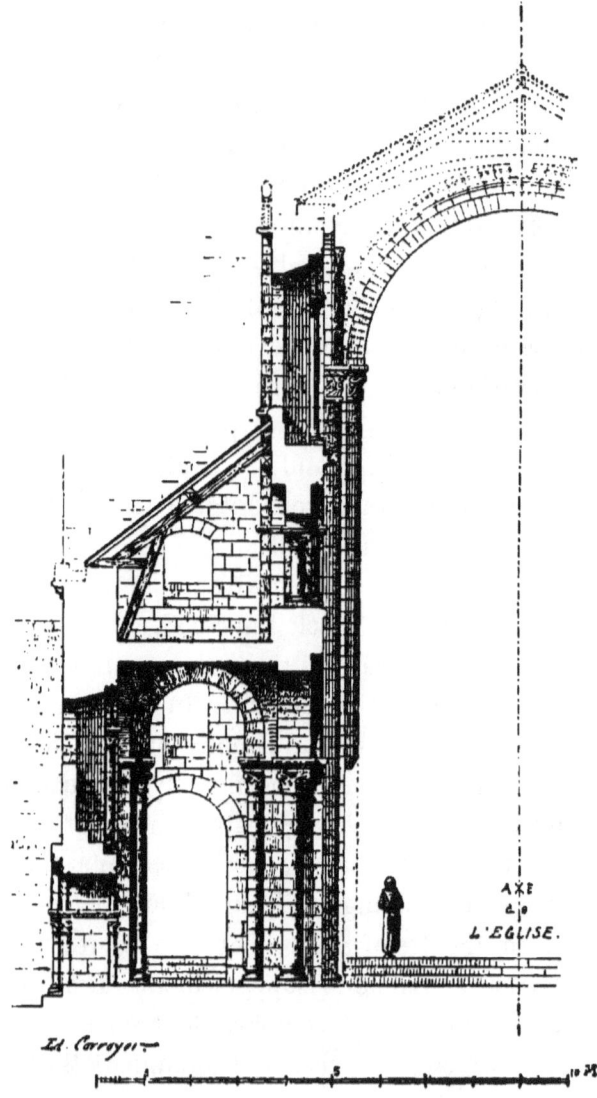

Fig. 33. — Nave. Transversal section on AB. (Present condition.)

Fig. 34. — Longitudinal section on CD. (Present condition).

arches of the south transept and of the west nave, calcined by the fire of 1834, have been newly plastered but not restored; they are terribly cracked especially those of the south, and they were obliged to place supports in January 1883, in order to avoid the threatening downfull.

CHANCEL

The romanesque chancel has entirely disappeared, and there does not exist any trace of its original form. It was probably, as we have seen in the historical notice, nearly like that of the church of Cerisy-la-Forêt, the apse of which still exists.

The present chancel was built from 1450 to 1521 on the enlarged site of the romanesque chancel, which fell down in 1421. Although it was constructed with very strong granite, like the other buildings of the Mount, it is very carefully formed and is a very good specimen of the edifices built during the last times of the pointed architecture. It seems to be evident that they wished in the XVth century, to rebuild entirely the church in the same style as the new chancel; this plan was commenced to be put in execution, and the intentions of the builders of 1450 are easy to be seen. This project is visible in the whole of the constructions and especially in the angles formed by the chancel and the transepts. In these places, the flying buttresses really sustaining the thrust of the vaults of the chancel cross each other with those of the projected transepts; these last flying buttresses, without reason and without object just now — A of the plan fig. 35 — have been only partially built

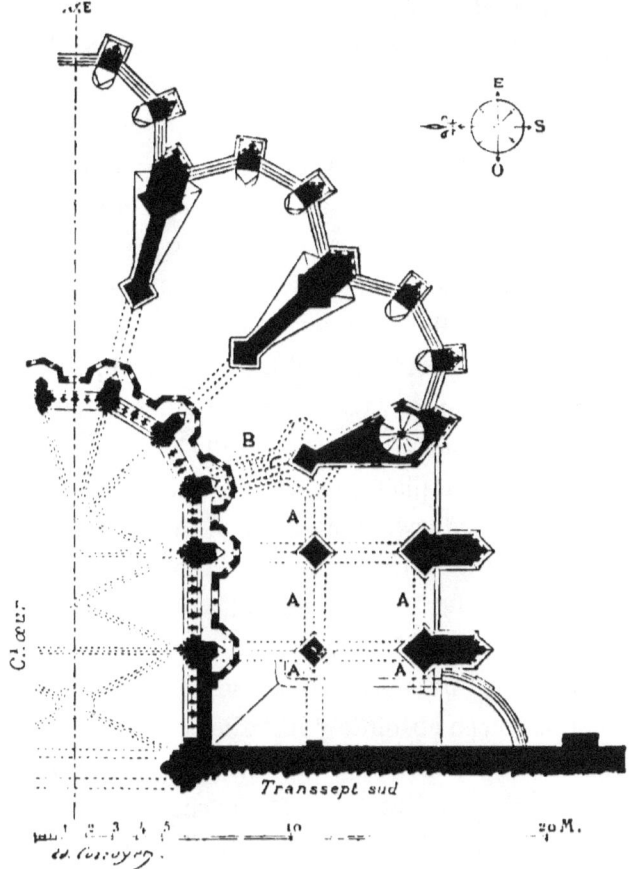

Fig. 35. — Chancel. Ground plan of the Triforium.

in anticipation of the further rebuilding of the transept according to the new plan.

We can judge of these arrangements by going round the chancel on the terraces of the apses of the chapels which we reach by the staircase built in the solid south buttress and the entrance of which is in the third south chapel.

The arrangement of this triforium is very ingenious; the exterior gallery goes round the supports on which it is constructed like corbels, in order to give them all the necessary strength, p'an, fig. 35, by forming on the base of the large windows and of the buttresses an architectural combination of a very nice effect.

The chancel is composed of a central nave, ended on the east by an apse with chamfers surrounded by an aisle around which extend and radiate lateral chapels with apses — see plan, fig. 22. — The chapels of the north side are narrower than those of the south and have a different form. This difference rendered necessary by the architecture, can be explained by the proximity of the buildings of the *Merveille*, which would have been spoilt by the north collateral, if this part of the church had been absolutely like the south one.

The construction of the chancel is very remarkable; the conception is grand and the execution a real masterpiece of that kind of architecture. The exactness and the regularity of the details show that perfect science and knowledge directed the geometrical operations which were necessary when its foundations were raised to the level of the soil. The perfection of the cut of the granite, the clearness of the most complex mouldings and the perfect sculptures show what art and what care were employed in the construction of these works.

After seeing the nave and the chancel, the visitor will be able to make an interesting ascent. By taking the staircase which we have already mentioned, in the third radiating chapel, he will reach the galleries of the triforium and, by ascending again the flight of steps built on the raking part of a flying buttress and called the *jagged staircase*, ending at the upper balustrade of the timber-roof, he will have before his eyes an immense panorama. He must afterwards go down by the same way to the foot of the staircase whence he ascended to the third chapel and which has its starting point in the lower church.

LOWER CHURCH CALLED CRYPT OF THE LARGE PILLARS

The difference between the level of the higher church and the exterior soil has necessitated the construction of considerable basements; they formed the *Lower church, called crypt of the large pillars*, which reproduces with great simplicity the arrangements of the chancel, except the lateral chapels of the first transverse compartment,

Fig. 36. — Chancel. — Section on the longitudinal axe.

which the rock prevented being made and those of
the second transverse compartment in the place of
which have been put *cisterns* made at the time of the
constructions in the depth of the substructures. The
plan, fig. 16, shows these dispositions in Y; the south
cistern is composed of two arcades, but the north has
only one. The pillars, round, thick and short, without
capitals receive by penetrations with corbels the coussinets of the vault and serve as the solid base for the
piers of the chancel of the higher church.

A fortified bridge, formerly having battlements and
which has still its machicolations, crosses the church
yard and makes the lower church communicate with
the abbatial dwelling on the south and the Merveille on
the north.

After visiting the lower church, the visitor ought
to go out on the north by the lateral door opening
on a narrow yard at the end of which is, towards
the east, a terrace whence he will admire the apse of
the church and the south front of the Merveille; afterwards he must ascend the staircase winding round that
terrace — R of the plan of the second zone, fig. 21 —
and which ends, on the level of the Guards'hall, in the
court of the Merveille, I of the plan fig. 20, 1st zone.

MERVEILLE

Nota. — In order to keep an exact remembrance of the *Merveille*, it is necessary to visit in the following order the two distinct buildings of which it is composed : from the court of the Merveille — I fig. 20 — the visitor enters by the Porch and the Gate which open at the foot of the tower of the Corbins — K fig. 21 — he will see the Almonry and the Cellar; he should ascend the staircase built in the thickness of the walls, in the south-west angle of the Cellar, and which ends on the first floor; he must observe the Knights' hall, and the Refectory; he must traverse the lateral gallery of the Knights' hall, which leads by turnings and staircases ending at the Cloister and the Dormitory which form the second floor.

The gigantic constructions, which rise on the north of the church, were called from their origin the *Merveille*.

This immense building, the most beautiful specimen which we have of the religious and military architecture of the middle ages, is composed of three floors : the lower one including the Almonry and the Cellar, the intermediate comprising the Refectory and the Knights' hall; the higher one containing the Refectory and the Cloister.

We must remark that it is formed of two edifices in

Page 84.

Fig. 15. — North front of the Merveille. Loisel.

juxtaposition and joined together, the one looking towards the east and the other towards the west. The former contains the Almonry, the Refectory and the Dormitory; the latter, *i. e.* the edifice of the west comprises the Cellar, the Knight's hall and the Cloister.

The Merveille was commenced in the XIIIth century, about 1203 and finished in 1228.

These splendid edifices, built entirely of granite, were erected at the same period, on a plan skilfully and powerfully imagined. We must admire this grand masterpiece when we think of the enormous efforts which were necessary to put it into execution so quickly *i. e.* in twenty-five years, on the side of a steep rock, separated from the continent by a moveable and dangerous shingle. In fact, this situation increased the difficulties of the transportation of the materials which were found in the quarries of the coast and from whence the monks brought the granit necessary to their works. A very small part of these materials was taken from the base of the rock itself; but if the crossing of the shingle was avoided, there were, however, great obstacles in using them after raising them to the foot of the Merveille, the base of which is more than 50 metres above the mean level of the sea.

Although some differences are to be noticed in the form of the exterior buttresses, resulting from the interior arrangements of the halls, yet it is not less certain

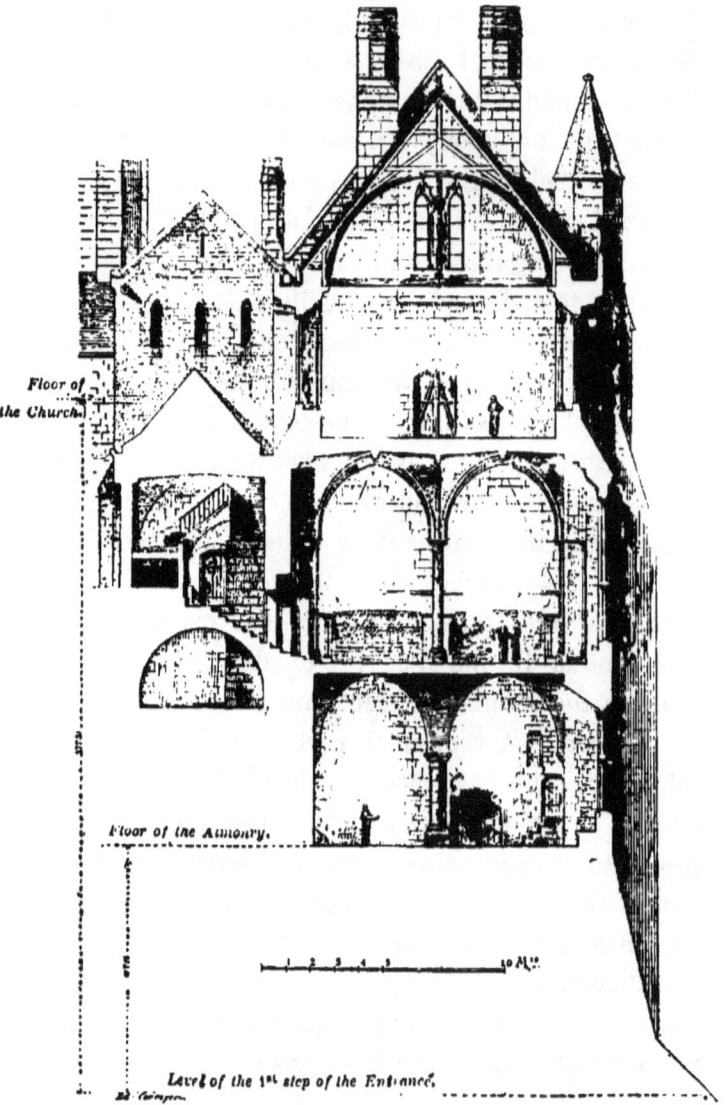

Fig. 38. — Merveille. — East edifices. — Transversal section from the south to the north.

Fig. 39. Merveille. — West edifices. — Transversal section from the north to the south. (Condition in 1872.)

that the two edifices composing the Merveille were planned and built at the same time. To be convinced of it, it is sufficient to study on the plans the sections and the façades, their general bearings and first of all he singular arrangement of the staircase built in the thickness of the buttress, at the point where these two buildings are joined together and crowned by a little octogonal tower; this staircase begins in the Almonry, ends in the Dormitory and the battlement above.

After these remarks and the *position* of the edifices having been explained, we continue their description, not in the order in which they were built, but in that which we have already stated. (See the note in *Merveille* intended to facilitate the visit of the halls of the Building.)

ALMONRY

The Almonry or alms' room, is composed of two naves. The roman plain groined vaults of a pointed form rest on a cluster of strong and thick columns the bases and the capitals of which are square. It is lighted by two small windows with deep bendings, pierced between the buttresses, two on the east and six on the north; they open out in the interior of the room and there are stone benches in the splayings.

The entrance door opens to the south on the court of

the Merveille. Under the porch, in front of it, is the starting point of a staircase contained in the tower, called Corbins' tower, K' of the plan fig. 21. This staircase, of great simplicity, but the construction of which is remarkable leads up to the Dormitory, to the higher south circular road and to the base of the timber-roof, after leading, half-way, to the battlement of the Chatelet and to the courtain which joins it to the Merveille.

During the researches made in 1872, by order of the Minister of public instruction and fine arts, we found near the south entrance door the remnants of a furnace and among the remains of burnt clay some pieces of melted white metal covered by green oxyde, indicating a mixture in which copper is present in large quantities. These are perhaps the remains of the bells melted in the Abbey or of the metal prepared to manufacture *obsidional* coins which the abbots of the mount were authorized to issue during the reign of Charles VII, at the period of the long wars with the English.

At the end of the Almonry, towards the west, there is a door communicating with the Cellar; this aparture with a double rabbet presents a peculiar arrangement being shut in by two leaves — one before the other — which, towards the Almonry were kept strongly closed each of them by a crossbeam fixed on one side in a mortice made on one of the doorposts and on the other side, in the wall, where, when the leaves were opened it was put, throughout the whole width of the door, in a square opening made for that purpose.

On the right of the double door is the entrance to the staircase constructed at the junction of the two buildings east and west; it leads to the Dormitory and above to the north battlement.

On the left, another door opens on a circular vertical conduit which makes the Almonry communicate with the Dormitory and which is used to bring up the water necessary to the monks for the service of the Dormitories, of the Vestry on the south and of the Lavatory situated in the south gallery of the Cloister.

CELLAR

The Cellar is formed by three naves with the roman plain groined vaults pointed and very acute in the two lateral naves rest on square pillars supporting the columns of the knights' hall above. It is lighted by five narrow pointed windows situated between the buttresses. Towards the west, a large door opens on the terraces and gardens below. It probably established communication between the Cellar and the Hall, built and destroyed, or simply began by Richard Tristan in the second half of the XIIIth century.

In the second transverse compartment, towards the west and under one of the windows, was placed a low door which opened on a draw-bridge made between the two buttresses — see section fig. 39 — and of which the arch which supported it when it was down can be still seen. This draw-bridge, making a projection on the front of the wall in order to kup its sloping base, was used to bring up, by a wheel placed in the Cellar, the water taken from the fountain Saint-Aubert, situated at the foot of the rock, and which was stored in the Cellar for the wants of the Abbey.

The Cellar was called *Montgommerie* or *Montgommery* since the unsuccessful attempt made by this partisan in 1591 to seize by surprise Mont Saint-Michel. We find in one of Dom Jean Huynes's manuscripts curious details of the attempts of the Huguenots during the wars of the League to seize upon the Abbey; from the incidents of this war we reproduce on of the most interesting episodes and which refers to the Cellar :

« Le gouverneur de Vicques estant mort, le sieur de Boissuzé fut instalé en sa place et, l'an 1591, attrapa les ennemys dans le piège qu'ils avoyent dressé pour le perdre selon que s'ensuit. Les Huguenots, tenant une grande partie de cette province de Normandie sous leur puissance et particulièrement les villes et chasteaux des environs de ce Mont, dressoient tous les jours des embusches pour envahir ce sainct lieu..... Il arriva un jour entre autres qu'ils prirent un des soldats et luy ayant desjà mis la corde au col, luy dirent que s'il vouloit sauver sa vie qu'il promît de leur livrer cet abbaye et que de plus ils lui donneraient une bonne somme de deniers. Cet homme, bien content de ne finir si tost ses jours et alléché de l'argent qu'ils luy promettoient, dit qu'il le feroit et convint avec eux des moyens de mettre cette promesse à exécution, qui furent que le soldat reviendroit en ce Mont, espieroit, sans faire semblant de rien, la commodité de les introduire secrettement en cette Abbaye et leur assigneroit le jour qu'il jugeroit plus commode pour cet effect. Le soldat leur ayant promis de n'y manquer, ils luy donnèrent cent escus et, bien résolu de jouer son coup, revint où il fut receu du Capitaine de Mont et des soldats sans aucun soupçon, puis se mit en devoir d'exécuter sa promesse. Pour donc la mettre à chef il advertit quelques jours après ces Huguenots de venir le vingt neufiesme de septembre, à huict heures du soir, jour de Dimanche et de la dédicace des églises Sainct-Michel, qu'ils montassent le long des degrez de la fontayne Sainct-Aubert; qu'estant là au pied de l'édifice il se trouveroit en la plus basse sale de dessous le cloistre, où, se mettant dans la roue (1), il en esleveroit quelques-uns des leurs qui par après luy ayderoient en grand silence à monter les autres. Ainsy

---

(1) Wheel fixed in the Cellar and used to bring up water near the draw-bridge which we have described before.

par cet artifice, ce Mont estoit vendu ; mais ce soldat, considérant le mal dont il alloit être cause, fut marry de sa lascheté et advertit le Capitaine de tout ce qui se passoit. Iceluy lui pardonna et se résolut avec tous ses soldats et autres aydes de passer tous ces ennemys par le fil de l'espée. Quant à eux, ne sçachant le changement de volonté de cet homme et se réjouissant de ce que le temps sembloit favoriser leur dessein, tant l'air estant ce jour remply d'espaisses vapeurs ; comme nous voyons arriver souvent, qui empeschoit qu'on les pût veoir venants de Courteil jusques sur ce rocher, ne manquèrent de se trouver au lieu assigné à l'heure prescrite. Alors le soldat faisant semblant qu'il estoit encore pour eux, se mit dans la roue et commença de les enlever l'un après l'autre, puis deux soldats de cette place les recevoient à bras ouverts, les conduisoient jusques en la salle qui est dessous le réfectoire, où ils leur faisoient boire plain un verre de vin pour leur donner bon courage, mais les menoient par après dans le corps de garde et ils les transperçoient à jour, se comportans ainsy consécutivement envers tous. Sourdeval, Mongomery et Chaseguey, conducteurs de cette canaille, s'esmerveilloient de ce qu'ils n'entendoient aucun tumulte, y en ayant desjà tant de montez, demandoient impatiemment qu'on leur jettast un Religieux par les fenestres afin de connoistre par ce signe si tout allait bien pour eux, ce qui poussa les soldats de ceans, desjà tout acharnez, de tuer un prisonnier de guerre qu'ils avoient depuis quelque jours lequel ils revestirent d'un habit de Religieux, puis lui firent une couronne et le jettèrent à ces ennemys. Mais, entrant en soubçon si c'estait un Religieux, Montgomery, voulant sçavoir la vérité, donna le mot du guet a un de ses plus fidelles soldats et le fit monter devant luy; estant monté en haut et ne voyant personne des siens il ne manqua de s'escrier: trahison! trahison! et de ce cry les ennemys prenant l'espouvante descendirent au plus fort du rocher, se sauvèrent le mieux qu'ils purent, laissant 98 soldats de leur compagnie, lesquels on enterra dans les grèves... »

On the right of the west gate, the staircase built in the thickness of the buttresses leads to the Knights' hall above.

KNIGHTS' HALL

The hall called Knights' hall — L of the plan fig. 21 — was begun in 1215 by Robert des Isles who died in 1218. Thomas des Chambres who succeeded him, finishedit about 1220. It was called Knights' hall only after the institution of the Order of Saint-Michel, established by Louis XI in 1469; it was used before as the Hall of the general assemblies or as that of the Chapter of the Abbey.

Besides, the general arrangements of the Knights' hall show it was destined for numerous meetings; what proves it, independently of its vast proportions, are the three *latrines* constructed especially and only for that hall; two stand on the north and outside, between the buttresses joined by arches. Each of them is preceded by a small *recess* communicating with the hall, lighted by two rows of trefoiled series of arches. — See fig. 37, north front of the Merveille. — A third *latrine* which is really the one for the old abbatial buildings of the XIst century and which was used by the builders of the XIIIth century, is in the south west angle. The visitor arrives there by a small chamfer door, and a passage built in the thickness of the west wall.

The Knights' hall is formed of four naves of unequal width; the first two rows of columns, towards the north, rest on the piers of the Cellar; the third row has its foundations on the rock. The vaults composed of transverse and pointed arches, adorned at their junction with a sculptered keystone, are supported by round columns with octogonal bases very finely cut; the capitals, richly and strongly sculptured are surmounted, as those of the Refectory by circular abacuses with high side faces deeply indented which have all the peculiar characters of the norman buildings of the XIIIth century.

Two large chimneys stand on the north front wall;

their large pyramidal mantels rise to the vault to which their summits are very cleverly joined. The flues of these chimneys go outside with a series of corbels ingeniously combined with the buttresses, the uppermost part of which they overtop, and their shafts crown the lateral wall of the Cloister.

Ed. Corroyer, del.

Fig. 40. — Knights' hall (XIIIth century).

The hall is lighted on the north by windows of different forms, and on the west by a large opening, now glazed; which used to communicate with the constructions (now in ruins), raised or only begun by Richard Tustin about 1260. On the south aisle, joining the romanesque substructures of the north transept is a lateral passage, standing at two metres above the level of the Hall, which makes a communication between the Refectory and the other parts of the Abbey, especially the Church, the Cloister, the Ambulatory and the west Substructures.

In the interior north-west angle, close to the staircase leading down to the Cellar, is the entrance to the Charter house, built on the exterior north-west angle of the Merveille. — L' of plan fig. 22. — The Charter house is composed of two small rooms placed one above the other, the first of which is alone vaulted; a winding staircase connects them inside; the end of the second floor is parallel with the west gallery of the Cloister, which is above the Knights' hall.

In the south east angle of the Hall, a door opens into the large porch which is in front of the Refectory. This porch, in the middle of which the Benedictine monks of the congregation of Saint-Maur placed, in 1650, a staircase which is shortly to be pulled down, opens, or rather, after the demolition of the staircase of the XVIIth century will open its arches to the north on a small court, in front of the north door of the lower Church. After descending some steps on the north we reach the Refectory.

REFECTORY

The Refectory commenced by Jourdain and finished by his successor Raoul des Isles, about 1215, is unquestionably the most beautiful hall of the Merveille — K in the plan fig. 21. — It is composed of a double nave the vaults of which formed by transverse and pointed arches, adorned at their junction by a sculptured rosette, and supported by a cluster of columns like those of the Almonry. The proportions of this hall, of which fig. 41 gives on idea are very well conceived and, according to the simplicity of the details of the architecture, the general effect is very grand.

The Refectory is lighted by nine large windows, contained in arcades formed by the lateral piers of the naves, the arches and the side-posts of the vaults; they rise to the top of the building and are separated by a mullion supporting an intermediate lintel, and there is a bench in their recesses.

In the north lateral part, beneath one of the windows, the lower glacis of which is higher than the other above the soil, *latrines* are very ingeniously established as well as the two *secret*, entrances, obliquely made in the thickness of the walls; they were covered by granite flag-stones, the toothings of which are per-

Éd. Corroyer, del.

Fig. 41. — Refectory (XIIIth century).

fectly distinct on the lateral fronts of the buttresses between which the *latrines* were established. The peculiar arrangement of the window above has perhaps made the local archeologists believe that the *pulpit of the Reader* stood in that place, this cannot be believed after examining the details of the constructions.

At the end of the Refectory, towards the west, on the wall which separates it from the Knights' hall, is a gigantic chimney with two hearths, the shafts of which crown the west gable of the Dormitory. Another chimney the traces of which are still seen, was made on the south side probably in the place where the Abbot and the guests of note dwelt. A stone pulpit does not exist as in many refectories of that period; it was probably a wooden one and it has been destroyed as well as the other ancient furniture of the Abbey.

On leaving the Refectory passing on the right under the Porch and taking the door on the left of the entrance to the Knights' hall, the visitor enters the Gallery which runs by the side of that hall and finishes with flights of steps to the old Cloister or ambulatory, — F of the plan fig. 21. — After ascending the staircase on the east end of this ambulatory, the visitor reaches the passage which leads : on the right to the north aisle of the romanesque church and on the left to the south Gallery of the Cloister.

CLOISTER

The Cloister commenced by Thomas des Chambres was finished by Raoul de Villedieu, in 1228. The general form is an irregular quadrilateral figure composed of four galleries which surround the discovered yard or *area of the Cloister* — L in the plan fig. 22.

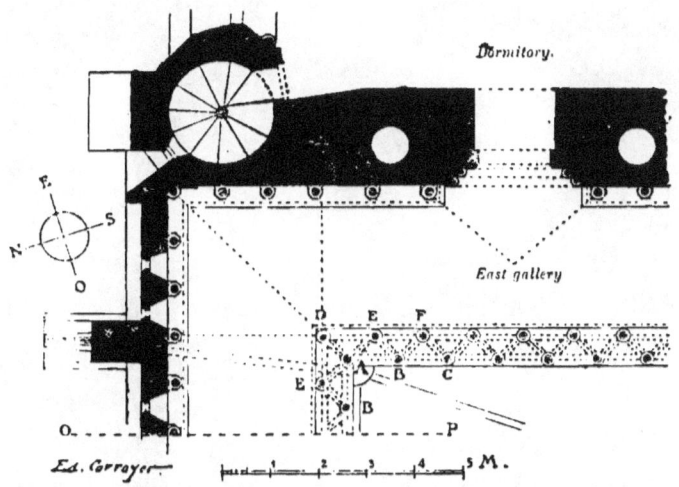

Fig. 42. — Cloister (XIIIth century). — Plan of the north-east angle.

The south gallery communicates with the Church and the old abbatial buildings of the XIth century, on the south-west restored and modified in the XIIth century, by Roger II.

9.

Fig. 13. — Cloister (XIIIth century). View taken from the west gallery.

The east one is joined to the Dormitory; the north one looks on the main sea, by small and low windows, let into the wall looking to the north, between the buttresses. Lastly the west one probably led to the Chapter, projected by Richard Tustin.

Of this Chapter, Richard only made the door, which opens on the west gallery and calls to mind, by its general composition, the entrance to the capitulary room of Saint-Georges de Boscherville.

At the angle of this last gallery, towards the north, — north-west angle of the Merveille, — the small door made in one of the lateral series of small arcades leads to one of the Halls of the Charter house, joined with the Knights' hall by an interior staircase.

« The Cloister of the Abbey of Mont Saint-Michel on sea, is one of the most curious and most complete of those we possess..... The series of arches is formed by two rows of small and narrow intermingling columns..... the archivolts with tierce points rest on the small columns from A to B, from B to C on the exterior, from D to F and from E to F in the interior, etc.; the triangles between the archivolts and the diagonal arches are filled like ordinary vault triangles fig. 43.

It is clear that this style of small columns forming a herse, resists more easily to the pressure and to the movement of timber works than the style of twin columns, in as much as the diagonal arches AD, AE, EB, etc., offer a double resistance to that pressure, prop the construction and make the two rows of columns of mutual support. Besides, we need not say that a weight

Fig. 44. — Cloister. Sculptured angle tie. (West gallery.)

resting on three feet is firmer than a weight resting on two or on four. Now, the gallery of the Cloister of the Abbey of Mont Saint-Michel is nothing but a suite of trivets..... The profiles of the ornamention call to mind the real norman architecture of the XIIIth century.

The capitals according to the anglo-norman fashion, are simply designed without foliage nor crockets round the corbeil. The capitals only of the series of arches placed against the wall are adorned by bastard crockets. The angle ties between the archivolts of the interior of the galleries offer beautiful sculptured fleurons in caissons, figures, a lamb overspread by a canopy; and, over the arches, a scrolled frieze or small roses finely worked. Between the bases of the diagonal arches of small vaults, crockets are sculptured. This Cloister was entirely painted, at least internally and in the two rows of small columns..... The galleries were primitively covered by timber-work with wainscots. (Viollet-le-Duc, *Dictionnaire raisonné de l'architecture française*, etc., tome III.)

In the south gallery, on the side parallel to the transept, the front of which was built by Raoul de Villedieu at the same time as the Cloister, is the *Lavatory*.

" It was at this fountain named the Lavatory that they (the monks) used to wash their feet at the time of certain ceremonies : *Omnes debent lavare pedes in claustro.* " It was also used to wash the bodies of the friars when they died; during this operation, all the monks placed themselves round (or before) the Lavatory, in the same order as in the chancel, in order to pray. " *Saint-Benoît's rules.* " (Albert Lenoir, *Monastic architecture.*)

As a rule, the Lavatory was near the Refectory this last joining the Cloister; but at Mont Saint-Michel where the steepness of the mountain did not allow the extension of the buildings by making them communicate together at the same level, it was necessary to put the halls one over the other and to change the ordinary arrangements of the regular benedictine monasteries.

Instead of being placed according to custom, either in one of the angles of the yard, or in of the fronts of the Cloister, the Lavatory was, on Mont Saint-Michel, established as near as possible to the Refectory, in the south gallery of the Cloister, on the exterior front of the north transept of the church; the base of this front forms two arcades joined to the striking buttresses by series of arches with rounded pendentives.

The Lavatory is composed of a double bench in each transverse compartment, the most elevated of which was used as a seat. Every double bench contains six places, *i. e.* in the two benches, twelve seats, without doubt arranged in remembrance of the twelve apostles.

Gutters, apparent on the elevated part of the higher benches, conducted water to the fountain which was provided with a small basin, built in the bottom of every lower bench.

The arrangements of the Lavatory permitted the monks to make their obligatory ablutions and to accomplish mutually the *washing of the feet*, which, according to the benedictine rules, had to be done in the Cloister, not only on holy Thursday, but also on every Thursday. " When it was very cold, in winter, and the water from the fountain placed in the Cloister was frozen, they went to the Dormitory to wash their feet and hands with hot water, which was brought there for that purpose. " (Albert Lenoir, *ditto*.)

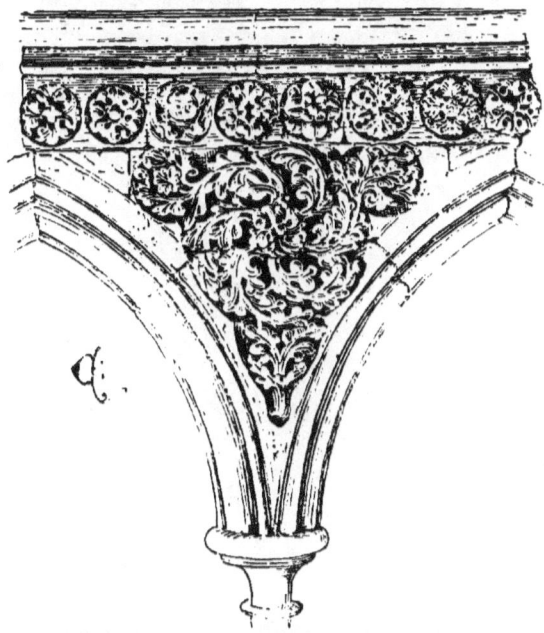

Fig. 45. — Cloister. Sculptured angle tie. (West gallery.)

In the interior of the galleries, the sculptured sketches adorning the angle ties are all different; the friezes too, although included in a known profile, are very rich, very varied, and all this sculpture, composed with the greatest cleverness, in executed with the highest perfection.

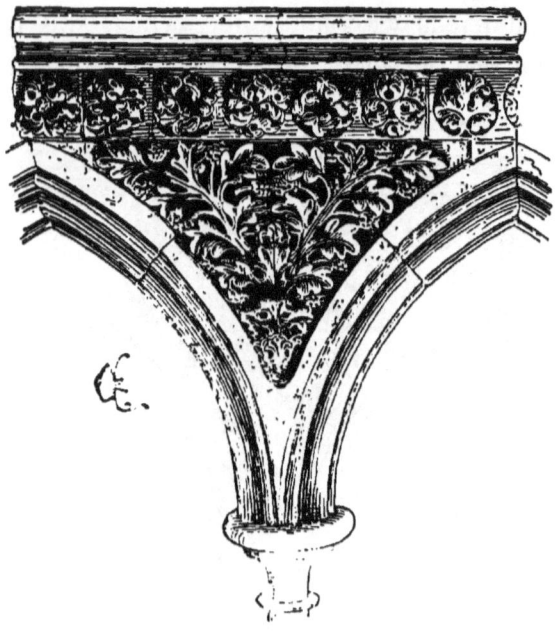

Fig. 16. — Cloister. Sculptured angle tie. (East gallery.)

In front of the doors, the Christ is figurated, according to the monastic fashion; on the east, opposite the principal door of the Dormitory, and on the west opposite the entrance to the Chapter the door of which has alone been built. On the south, rather on the right of the door, the Christ is on a throne, formed by a small and very thin column with its capital adorned with flowers, and accompanied by two figures. The higher part of the angle tie is adorned with three gables, very nicely sculptured, forming a canopy above

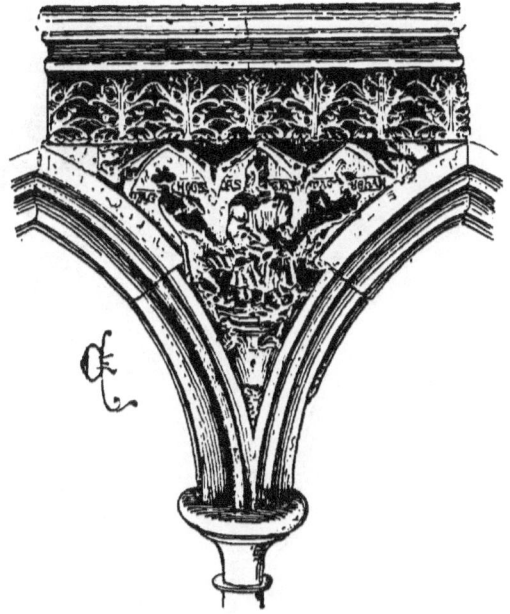

Fig. 47. — Cloister. Sculptured angle tie. (South gallery.)

the Christ and the lateral figures; the state of mutilation of this last basso relievo prevents you from discerning clearly (except the figure of the Christ blessing) the subject of the composition, but that which renders it particularly interesting are the names engraven on each side of the heads, or, more accurately the places which they occupied. They are without doubt the names of the architects or sculptors of the Cloister: Maître Roger, Don Garin and Maître Jehan.

Fig. 48. — Cloister. Sculptured angle tie. (South gallery.)

The exterior arcades, on the Area of the Cloister, internally sculptured are in Caen stone; it is the only place in the Abbey were calcarious stone has been used. In spite of its weakness and the mouldings of its arches very much excavated, this stone rather soft, resisted the salinous wind, except however in one part of the east and north faces, where the south-west winds, from the open sea, have deeply altered it.

The Area of the Cloister forms, in a large part of its extent, the covering of the Knights' Hall, — see the section figure 39; — the declivities, transversely made, send the rain-water outside by canals which cross the north galleries of the Cloister and end in gargoyles, placed on the exterior buttress of the north front. From the XVth century, the water was collected and sent into the cistern of the north aisle of the chancel rebuilt after its destruction in 1421 and commenced about 1450, by the cardinal Guillaume d'Estouteville.

The Cloister has been lately restored by the cares of Ministry of public Instruction and Fine Arts, on the recommendation of the commission of historical buildings. The works made under our direction were commenced in 1877 and entirely finished in 1881.

The thin columns of the exterior series of arches as well as the capitals and the bases are of *granitel* turned and polished, like the rare specimens which have been fortunately preserved and which have been faithfully reproduced in all their details.

The *granitel* is found in the neighbourhood of *Luzerne d'Outre-Mer* (Manche); the quarries were worked from .

the XIIth century, and the Abbots of the old and celebrated Abbey of Luzerne often used them to make presents, especially to the Benedictine monks of Mont-Saint-Michel, with whom they were in very cordial relations in the XIIIth century at the time of the construction of the Cloister.

It was very interesting to find available for the restoration the same materials which had been used for the primitive construction; and after our numerous searches in order to find the old quarries the layers of which had been indicated to us by historical records about Mont-Saint-Michel, this result has been attained thanks to the good will of the proprietor, the count Henry de Canisy who wished to follow the good example formerly given by the old landlords of the Abbey of Luzerne.

The timber-roof of the galleries has been restored according to the most certain data furnished by pieces of the ancient timber work found in the roofs which have been very often modified especially by the Directors of the Prison; these records have permitted giving to the vaults which cover the galleries their primitive form which is very beautifully and very beautifully designed so as not to overcharge the light and graceful series of arches on the exterior.

In the east gallery, a fine and large door in connexion with the interior arcades which run at the back of the exterior walls of the Cloister leads into the Dormitory, the apartments belonging to which communicated by a small door with the south gallery.

DORMITORY

At the same time that he finished the Knights' Hall, Thomas des Chambres ordered the building of the Dormitory which he finished before his death, about 1225.

The Dormitory is a large Hall erected above the Refectory of which it has the same general dimensions; but, instead of being, as the latter, vaulted with stones and divided into two parts, it was in one, and covered with timber-work. The evidence of that primitive arrangement is seen in the west gable-end still standing entire; the stone wall arch which supported the semicircular wainscot, still exists and attests the ancient form.

The Dormitory is lighted, on the north and on the south, by a succession of small windows, long and narrow, having the form of loop-holes; their apertures widen towards the outside and their crownings, by their peculiar forms in bee nests, seem to be a reminiscence of oriental art, seen by the French crusaders during their expeditions in Palestine. In the interior, these windows having their apertures widened the same as the outside are framed by small columns supporting fine series of arches surmounted by a projecting cornice, on which rested the wainscotted barrel-vaulting. On the east, two large windows light the eastern end of the Dormitory.

On the west, the principal door of the Dormitory opens on the east gallery of the Cloister; a lateral door opens on the same side and leads to the Church by the south gallery of the Cloister running parallel with the north transept. Towards the south-west angle, a door makes communication between the Dormitory, the Vestry and the Warming place and with the Cloister by a small door on the west. In the opposite angle on the north west, ends the winding staircase, built in the thickness of the buttress at the junction of the two buildings of the Merveille, which having its starting point in the Almonry, ends above, on the north battlement the toothings of which are still seen on one of the sides of the small tower crowning the staircase.

In the south front, very nearly in the middle, is a large niche including two series of arches, planned and built from the beginning as is proved by all the details of the construction. There were placed the lamps formed by holes dug in a stone and so disposed as to receive a wick or a wax ball, furnished with a wick, the consumption of which enabled one to juge approximately what was the time, or, finally, any light which, according to Saint-Benoît's rules, was to be burnt all night in the Dormitory: "*Candela jugiter in eadem cella ardeat usque mane*" Albert Lenoir, *Monastic architecture.* — According to this same rule, the monks should lie down in their clothes — *vestiti dormiant* (*ditto*) on separate beds and, as much as possible, in the same room : *Monachi singuli per singula lecta dormiant, si potest fieri, omnes in una loco dormiant* (*ditto*)." Also the plans made by the first builders show clearly that the Dormitory, was in the XIIIth century, established according to the regular customs of the Benedictine monks. At this time, " the Dormitories, as a rule, had no ceiling (or were not vaulted) and the beams overhead were visible (*ditto*). "

In the XVth century, contrary to the old rule, the Dormitory was divided into cells, according to the orders which Pierre le Roy, before starting for his long journey, gave the claustral Prior of the Abbey, Dom Nicolas de Vandastin.

The timber-roof of the Dormitory was several times fired. In 1300, the lightning struck the Church the roof of which was burnt, as well as that of the Dormitory. Guillaume du Château repaired the damage during the time he had the control of the Abbey. In 1374, the lightning again set fire to the Church and the Dormitory, several lodgings of the Monastery and almost all the houses of the Town; Geoffroy de Servon began the restoration of the Dormitory which was finished in 1391 by Pierre le Roy, who rebuilt the pyramid of the octagonal Tower of the Refectory, called : Corbins Tower. " Having restored the temple, he took care of the Monastery : he ordered the Tower of the Refectory, to be rebuilt which had fallen down some time before. " (Don Jean Huynes.)

From this time (end of the XIVth century) till the beginning of the XVIth century the Dormitory as well as the buildings of the Monastery were carefully attended to, but during the time of the commendatory Abbots, the building and restoring were discontinued. Several decrees of the Norman parliament were necessary to make the Abbots do the necessary repairs.

In the midst of difficulties of every kind with which the Abbey was troubled, such a looseness of manners in the morals of the Monks caused them to be replaced in 1622 by the monks of Saint-Maur; the new inhabitants of Mont Saint-Michel unhappily spoilt the Dormitory. In 1629 this magnificent hall was divided into two parts by the establishment of new cells, and under the pretext of lighting, they enlarged the interior recesses of the windows by undermining the thin columns which framed them and the series of arches which crowned them.

The transformation of the Abbey into a prison, profaning the Church and the sacred places, increased the already mutilated ruins. Like the other halls of the Monastery profanely inhabited, the Dormitory was divided into two floors of rooms for the prisoners and over was a loft; on the north front, foul *latrines* were built which were happily pulled down last year. The actual roofing is modern; above the *wall arch* about which we spoke before, on the interior front of the west gable are seen the projecting listels destined to prevent the infiltration of rain water between the wall and the covering; they determine surely the primitive form of the old gable-end and timber-roof.

The halls of the Merveille, except the Cellar and the interior galleries of the Cloister, were paved in terra cotta square panes, coloured and enamelled, some remnants of which we have collected in the excavations which were made in diverse parts of the Abbey.

The timber-roof of the Dormitory was covered with varnished tiles; we have also found some pieces of those tiles in the ruins of the flight of steps leading to the fountain Saint-Aubert.

The restoration of the Dormitory commenced in 1882, thanks to the new and important credits opened by the Ministry of public Instruction and Fine-Arts, will be finished in four or five years.

The Cloister and the Dormitory are on the top of the Merveille; if the visitor has followed us, he will have thoroughly seen this, or rather, those magnificent buildings.

On descending the staircase of the Corbins' tower, which communicates with the Dormitory by a small door in the south east angle, the visitor must stop halfway to see the battlement of the Chatelet, which is just as it was in the XVth century; besides we will refer to this later, on leaving the Abbey; afterwards, in descending, he will come again under the porch at the entrance of the Almonry; but before leaving the Merveille, it seems to us necessary to say some words about the works which protected it on the north, as well as about the fountain Saint-Aubert, which had a considerable importance from the XIIIth to the XVth century.

FORTIFICATIONS OF THE MERVEILLE
FOUNTAIN SAINT-AUBERT

Independently of its formidable fronts, which can be considered as veritable fortifications, the Merveille was protected by an embattled wall joined to the ramparts. This wall was flanked by a tower, also with battlements, which was used as a parade ground for the circular roads extending towards the west. In the middle, at the level of the north-west angle of the Merveille, a small Chatelet, now destroyed, protected the very steep flight of steps, which was closed by embattled walls, which led down to the fountain Saint-Aubert.

This fountain stands on the north at the lower part of the rock. We have seen, in the historical notice, the details which Don Jean Huynes gives about the miraculous origin of this fountain, which was surrounded by a high tower and from there to the lower halls under the Cloister, you can see a large flight of steps, closed by walls, etc.

A great part of the staircase of the fountain still exists. Under the bushes and the crumbling ground, we found its steps, the bases of its lateral walls, and at its lowest end the traces of a circular construction and ruins of the fortified Tower, built about the middle of the XIIIth century, to contain the precious fountain.

Till the time when Guillaume d'Estouteville ordered the two large cisterns to be built in lower collaterals of the new Chancel, rebuilt from the XVth to the XVIth century and commenced by this abbot in 1450, the *high tower* of which Dom Jean Huynes speaks included the only fountain of Mont Saint-Michel. It is easy to understand that it was indispensable to protect it, firstly against the sea which invaded it during high water, and afterwards against the attempts which the enemy made to seize it. The Tower of the fountain fortified, joined to the works of the Abbey by the embattled staircase, was one of the principal parts of the exterior defences of the place. Beyond the necessity to preserve the fountain, the Tower made an advanced post very important in a strategical prospect, because the situation of the work permitted the garrison to be supplied from the sea. It is assuredly in this place, accessible during full tide; that the Abbey received the supplies from the Duke of Britanny when, at the end of the year 1423 and at the beginning of 1424, Mont Saint-Michel was blocked by land and by sea.

Resuming our itinerary, hindered by a useful digression, we must cross the yard taken before entering the Merveille. After visiting on the left one of the floors of the Chatelet, which is actually the office of the guardians of the Fine-Arts — (faithful guardians, punctual and unbiassed, whom the visitors, more and more numerous, value according to their merits) — we shall find ourselves again in the Guards' Hall and, after descending the steps which we took on arrival, in the Barbican from whence we shall be able to admire the Chatelet forming the Door of the Abbey, the entrance of which it protects — see fig. 19.

CHATELET

During the first part of the XVth century, Pierre le Roy built the Chatelet and the Curtain joining that work to the Merveille by means of the Corbins' tower : « And from this tower to Belle-Chaise he ordered the wall which is seen there to be built. Near it was constructed the dungeon above the flight of steps at the entrance of the Guard-house. » (Don Jean Huynes.)

He also constructed the Barbican, comprising the sally port of the Chatelet and the Door of the Abbey, as well as the large flight of steps on the north side and the staircase on the south.

The Chatelet (dungeon) was built in front of the north external front of Belle-Chaise, on which it leans without joining, leaving between this front and the south one an empty space, a large machicolation protecting the northen door, which has become the second inward door since the Chatelet has been constructed. It comprises a square building, which contains in the angles of the north front, two little towers with corbels, resting on buttresses and which look, like two immense bombards, standing on their breeches. Between the pedestals of those small towers is the door, where are the stairs — leading to the Guards' Hall — which were protected by a portcullis worked from the interior to the first floor of the Curtain joining the two small towers.

The Chatelet includes as well as the raking-vault of the staircase, a nook left between that vault and the floor of the first room — now the guardians' office, in the court of the Merveille — and in which was the loop-hole pierced above the Door; three floors lighted on the east and on the north and each of them was provided with a chimney the top of which rises above the roof.

The wall or Curtain joining the Merveille and the Chatelet built at the same time as this last building, gives internally on the court of the Merveille the toothings of a planned building, the door and the postern of which alone were finished, on the north front of Belle-Chaise and looking on the court of the Merveille of which they were to make the entrance. This construction was not finished as is proved by the state of the wall arches of the lower part, which was probably vaulted.

The Chatelet and the Curtain are admirably built of granite; their stones forming grey and pink lines alternately to the height of the first floor (of the Chatelet only) as well as the profiles of the mouldings, are cut with the greatest perfection. By these means they are very well conserved, and, except the necessary rebuilding of the timber-roof, ruined in part, it is possible to put them in their primitive state without very important works.

The perspective view taken from the north door of the Barbican, figures the entrance to the Abbey in its actual condition, except the battlement of the Barbican which is supposed to be rebuilt — fig. 19. It shows : the Chatelet, the door of which opens between the buttresses supporting the small towers, where begins the flight of steps which ascends to the Guards' Hall (Belle-Chaise) and, on the right of the figure, the Curtain joining the Chatelet to the Merveille; on the left, the south door of the Barbican.

BARBICAN OF THE CHATELET

LARGE FLIGHT OF STEPS ON THE NORTH AND STAIRCASE ON THE SOUTH

The Barbican surrounding the Chatelet on the east and on the north, forms a first line of defence the battlement of which is reached by a small staircase. An embattled watch-tower stands in the south east angle near the south door — M fig. 49 — it is provided with a chimney with machicolations, and was used as a shelter for the military guardians of the two doors of the Barbican.

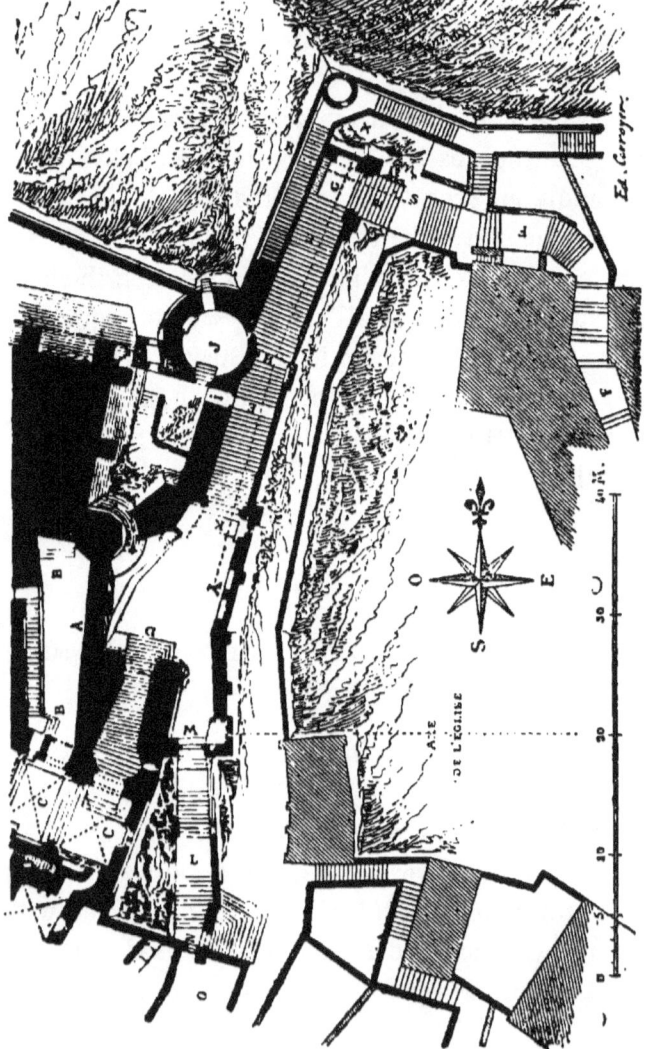

Fig. 49. — Plan of the exterior defences of the entrance to the Abbey. — Barbican of the Chatelet. Large flight of steps on the north and staircase on the south.

EXPLANATORY NOTE

- A   Curtain joining the Chatelet to the Merveille.
- B   Court of the Merveille.
- C   Guards' Hall.
-     First step of the entrance to the Abbey.
- E   Large flight of steps. — Stair head communicating with the postern I.
- F   Fligth of steps continuing the slopes of the streets of the town.
- G   First fortified door of the first flight of steps.
- H   Second fortified door   ditto.
- I   Postern opening on the Claudine tower J and on the Ramparts by the staircase on the left.
- J   Claudine tower. — Guard-house.
- K   Third fortified door of the large flight of steps. — North door of the Barbican.
- L   South staircase.
- M   South door of the Barbican. — On the right of the staircase, guard-house on the level of the Barbican.
- N   Postern communicating with the circular roads on the south.
- O   Circular roads.

" In front of the door of the Abbey were sometimes established advanced military works, in order to render more difficult the approach of the assailants, as would have been done before a fortress : those were barbicans which, in the case of an attack gave time to prepare for the defence and to close the gates. A remarkable specimen of those first military works was to be seen at Saint-Jean-des-Vignes, at Soissons (barbican of a rectangular form having a great analogy with that of Mont Saint-Michel). These advanced constructions — barbicans, — which were established in the middle ages in front of a place, were equivalent to the works named *tête de pont*, *demi-lune* (or *ravelin*) in the modern fortifications. » (Albert Lenoir, *monastic architecture*.)

LARGE FLIGHT OF STEPS AND STAIRCASE ON THE SOUTH

Two staircases lead to the Barbican : the north one is the large flight of steps, very wide, the steps of which are very low, and form the suite of the slopes of the street of the town, ending at the exterior defences of the Castle. The large flight of steps is established in a parallel with the west rampart, but without any communication with it; formerly a fortified door stood on the lower part of the stairs; a second door stopped the passage half-way, on a landing place where a small postern on the level of the landing place communicating with a guard house built in the lower part of the Claudine Tower, allowed the military to go on the flight of steps at the first signal. Lastly was a third door opening into the Barbican.

The south staircase is not so important; it established the necessary communications between the Barbican and the outside part by a postern built on the foot of the staircase and the exterior circular roads leading to the Barbican.

The figure 50 shows the condition of the large flight

of steps in 1872, by a longitudinal section made parallel with the line XY of the plan fig. 49 (in the direction of the two letters turned upside down).

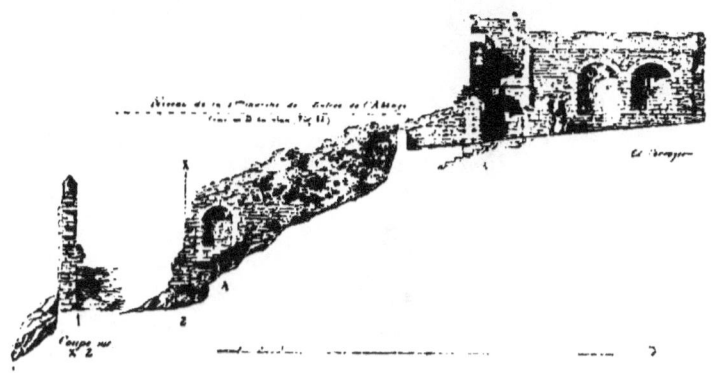

Fig. 50. — Large flight of steps. — Longitudinal section on XY.
(Condition in 1872.)

These traces give incontestable proofs of the primitive dispositions which we have reestablished in the following drawing (fig. 51).

The figure 51 shows the longitudinal section made by following the line XY of the plan fig. 49; the large flight of steps is reestablished as well as the first door; this one, the intermediary door and the Barbican door, are provided with folding sides parallel with the flight of steps.

This large flight of steps so powerfully fortified by nature and by military art, was entirely independent of the Ramparts with which it could however communi-

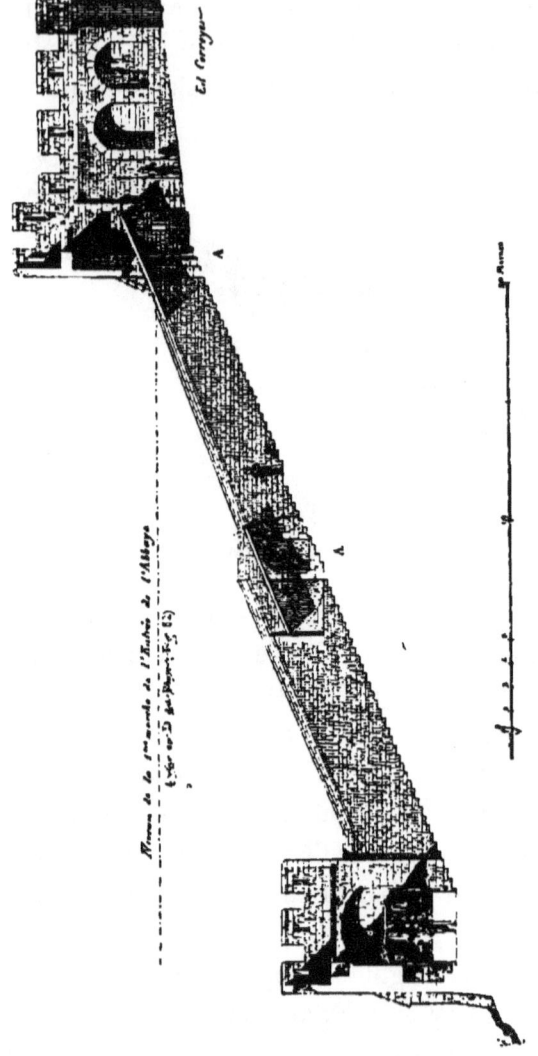

Fig. 51. — Large flight of steps. — Longitudinal section on XY. — Restoration.

cate, for the needs of the defenders, but only by a narrow postern opening on the large flight of steps, the passage of which was easily intercepted. The ramparts on the west and on the north, rose above the large flight of steps, and made it easy to be defended. A great part of those works still exist and the study of their traces is especially interesting, because all these special dispositions form a scarce and perhaps the only specimen of the military architecture in the middle ages.

The two doors of the large flight of steps and the two north and south entrances to the Barbican were each closed by only one leaf, of the same size as the openings, and which was horizontally moved and worked by a particular system which is explained by the exceptional situation of Mont Saint-Michel the edifices as well as the works of which are placed one over the other and are joined together only by a series of flight of steps and slopes of various kinds.

The leaves of the doors turned on their horizontal axis resting on projecting doorposts, established inside of the doors; they were opened in a parallel manner with the declivity of the flight of steps (A fig. 50 and 51) and at the least alert, it was easy to let them down very quickly, for they were pulled down by the weight itself of the lower part provided with heavy iron-works; they were kept shut by bolts, laterally fixed on the interior part of the leaves : the staples of the locks of which are still seen sealed in the posts of the doors.

The shut leaves made great opposition to the attacks from the exterior, because supported by the lateral rebates and the interior steps, directed against the pressure, they could not be broken through or driven up except after long attempts: by these means they defied any surprise.

The skilful means used to protect the approches of the Barbican of the Chatelet, as well as the obstacles accumulated on the stairs which lead to its doors, detained the assailant and counteracted the attempts which he made to seize, by an attack with open force, upon the exterior works of the gate of the Fortress-Abbey. Therefore, thanks to its protectors and principally to its abbots, clever architects as well as vigilant captains, the military work of whom completed the natural defences which rendered it inexpugnable, the Abbey had the glorious and rare honour of resisting victoriously the violent assaults of the Englishmen as well as the perfidious artifices of the Huguenots, and has never been the prey of the enemies of France and of the catholic religion.

We give the figure 52, which shows the fronts of the edifices built from the XIIIth to the XVth century, as well as those of the Barbican, the plan of which is detailed in figure 49.

he Abbey. — Restoration. Page 130.

Fig. 56. — East front of the Merveille and of the edifices at the entrance to the Abbey. — Restoration. Page 130.

RAMPARTS

On going out by the north gate of the Barbican of the Chatelet and taking on the left the line of Ramparts, teh visitor will reach the small parade, in front of the *Claudine Tower* which commands and protects, by machicolations, the passage leading from the large flight of steps and from the Ramparts to the north circular roads, see plan fig. 49. From the elevated position, he will be able to judge the dispositions of the large flight of steps of which we have just spoken.

After descending a first slope on the west, — which ends in a watch-tower forming the projecture of the walls, and afterwards a second slope on the north, where stands the North Tower, from which the visitor will enjoy a series of magnificent sights, most of the whole of the Edifices of the Merveille and of the Abbey, or the immense panorama of the high sea, of Tombelaine and of the coasts and shingles, or the greatest part of the walls extending on the east and on the south of the Town and of the Abbey.

The North Tower, forming the north east projecture of the Ramparts, exists still in great part, uncrowned and filled in by ground and refuse of every kind; but we hope that it will be soon cleared and purified as was, in these last years, the small bastil of the Boucle Tower.

The North Tower offers, by its general arrangements, its loopholes and the details of its structure, all the particularities of the military architecture of the time when it was built (1255 to 1260). At first it was not covered by machicolations. This system was established only in the first part of the XIVth century, when all the defences were on the top of the walls; in the place of the wooden *parapets*, only put there during the war and often fired by the assailants, were placed stone *parapets* or *machicolations* with embattled parapets, equally of stone.

Guillaume du Château (1299-1314) increased the fortifications of the town and finished them when he governed the Abbey. In 1300, the fire which caused so much damage to the buildings of the Abbey, had reached the town and burnt to the ground almost all of its dwellings; Guillaume restored the monastery and rebuilt the houses of the town by means of help sent by Philippe le Bel after this monarch came as a pilgrim to Mont Saint-Michel. It is about this time that Guillaume du Château continued building the Ramparts commenced by Richard Tustin, by enlarging the east front of the fortress towards the South and joining its walls to the rugged sides of the rock on which are erected the abbatial edifices.

Ramparts erected by Guillaume du Château a part of the curtains, and some of the brackets forming the machicolations still exist; these traces are apparent on the east in the actual ramparts, on the right between the North Tower and the *Bastillon* of the Boucle Tower. The five brackets which are seen there — at least in 1872 and within the last few years, — are composed of three corbels put one over the other, roughly cut, but placed in order so as to firmly support the stone parapet, according to the system of defence newly invented and leaving between each bracket a large machicolation, much larger than those which were made in the XVth century. The wall of the curtain, above the brackets rests on a sloping base, in order to increase the violence of the missiles rebounding on this bank.

The door of the Enclosure built by Guillaume, in the beginning of the XIVth century, was probably on the east and south-east, and very likely at the place where the rock, by allowing landing and rather easy access, necessitated defensive works, between which opened the entrance to the town.

Nothing remains of the arrangements of that time. There only exist some parts of walls on the east side, in the interior of the present ramparts; but they only indicate the direction of the Ramparts without specifying the exact place of the old Gate. We must however consider in a certain manner the traditional records which put the Gate of the old Ramparts of the Town on the east in front of Avranches. We read in a part of the manuscripts left by Thomas le Roy, about the works of Robert Jolivet : « La Porte de la ville fut changée. Estant vis-à-vis de l'Église parocchiale, elle fut mise où elle est à présent. » A manuscript of the beginning of the XVth century gave us very important records about this matter as well as of the old Ramparts. The *breviary of Pierre II, duke of Britany*, contains a great number of miniatures and that which adorns the page of Saint-Michel's office represents independently of the figure of the Archangel a very curious illustration especially by the information which it gives us about Mont Saint-Michel at the end of the XIVth century — fig. 1.

On leaving the platform of the North Tower, and descending the very steep flights of steps crowning the walls, we reach the angle formed by the walls of the XIVth century and those which Robert Jolivet erected from 1415 to 1420.

At that time, the town was enlarged towards the south, and independently of the necessity of protecting it against the Englishmen intrenched in Tombelaine, it was necessary to oppose the attack with a much stronger defence than the ramparts of the XIVth century. This new arrangement, if more defenders were necessary in the fortress, obliged the enemy to extend his lines. Robert Jolivet put his new walls on the east against those of Guillaume du Château. Afterwards descending the steepness of the rock, protected by the North Tower, to the shingle, he flanked his walls, at first by a Tower changed into a *Boulevard* or *Bastillon* in the XVIth century, forming a considerable projecture destined to reach the sides of the adjacent curtains and to protect the front of the work as well as the place;

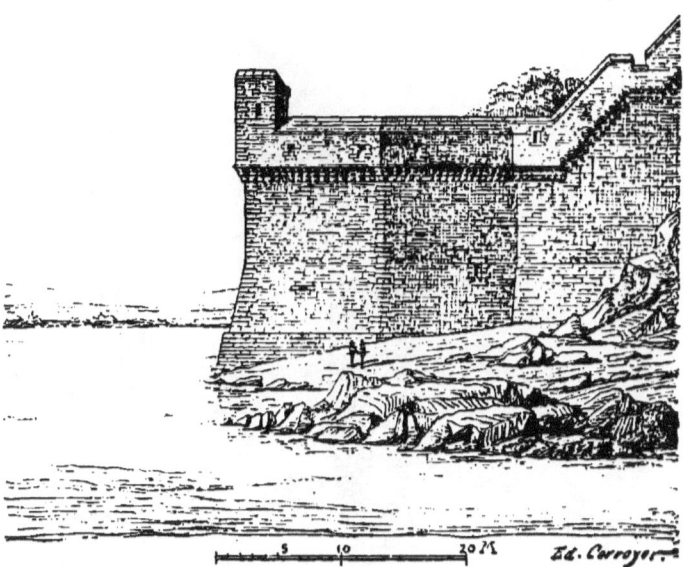

Fig. 53. — Boulevard (or *Bastillon*) on the East. — North side.

afterwards, he continued the walls on the south strengthening them by five other towers, one of which he placed at the obtuse angle formed by the curtains.

The last Tower, called King's Tower, forms the south-west projecture of the Place and protects at the same time the Gate of the Town, King's Gate. From this point the ramparts turning at a right angle, are joined by staircases and embattled circular roads, overlooked

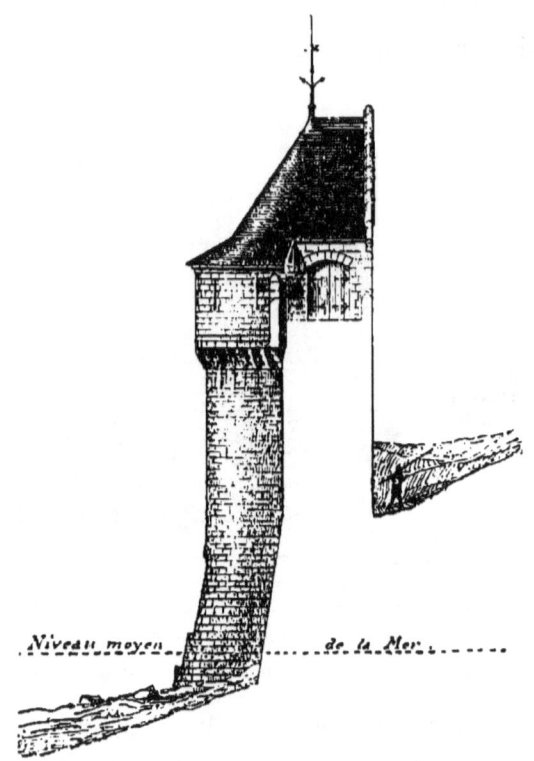

Fig. 54. — Ramparts of the XVth century. (Section of the walls.) North side of the Boucle Tower.

by a guard-house, to the steep slopes of the inaccessible rock, the fortified tops of which, communicate with the defences of the Abbey on the south.

The walls and their sloping bases are protected by

Fig. 55. — Ramparts of the XVth century. (Boucle Tower.) Front of the East posterns.

machicolations placed on the top the brackets of which support exposed and embattled parapets.

By continuing to go down and follow the crowning of the ramparts of the XIVth century and those of the XVth century, we will successively see : the Bastillon of the Boucle Tower — repaired or simply drained in 1880, — the interior arrangements of which can be studied; the Boucle Tower, shown in the figures 54 and 55; the arms of Robert Jolivet which adorn a niche built, — L of fig. 55 — in the east curtain, joining the Boucle Tower; the *low Tower* or *low battery*, *terraced* and disposed in a *barbette battery* in the XVIIIth century; the Tower called *Liberty's Tower* which is as the North Tower and the Bastillon of the Boucle Tower, filled with earth and the higher terrace of which was changed into a kitchen-garden; the *Arcade* or Squadron Tower, which preserved its primitive form and is overtopped by the adjoining buildings of a guard-house the curious front of which we have already seen — fig. 12 — on entering the town, the visitor will be again at the Gate of the Town — King's Gate — which is worthy of his attention.

The Gate of the Town, King's Gate, built at the same time as the walls and the East and South Towers, by Robert Jolivet, is on the west front of the place.

Its approaches are protected, beyond the Barbican, by the King's Tower and embattled walls established on

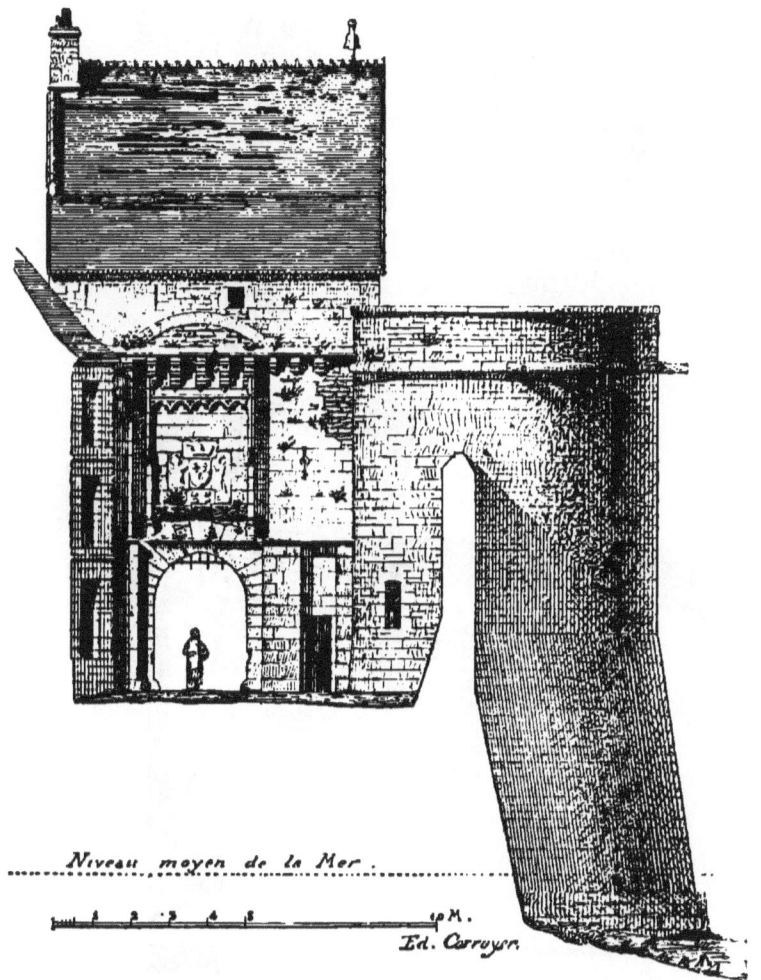

Fig. 56. — Ramparts of the XVth century. — King's Gate.
West front. (Condition in 1872.)

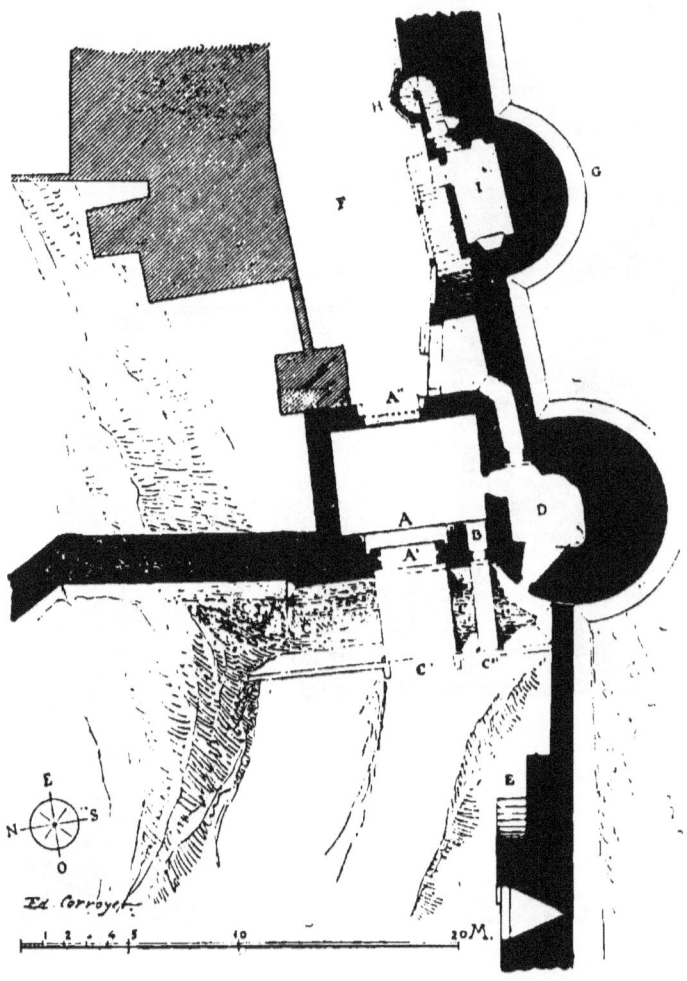

Fig. 57. — Ramparts of the XVth century. — Plan of the Entrance to the Town.
King's Gate.

EXPLANATORY NOTE

- A   Principal door.
- A'   Grooves of the portcullis.
- A"   Interior door towards the Town.
- B   Postern.
- C   Ditch.
- C' and C" Drawbridges.
- D   King's Tower (first guard-house of the Town). Above a similar building joining the King's dwelling.
- E   Curtain of the Barbican.
- F   Street of the Town.
- G   Squadron or Arcade Tower.
- H   Watch-Tower. — Above and sideways, I, a second guard-house of the Town.

the slopes and tops of the rock overlooking the Barbican and the Entrance into the Town. This gate is a very interesting work. Built in granite, as all the Edifices and the Ramparts of the Mount, it is composed with great art and made with very great care, though it follows the numerous exigencies of the military defences. Preceded by a ditch on which the drawbridges fell, they formed a first defence when they were drawn up. The principal Gate, for the use of carts, and the lateral postern lead to the Town. Above the doors is the dwelling of the doorkeeper or *King's Dwelling*, he is the commander of the door, keeping it for the king.

The principal passage and that of the corresponding postern are on the level with a first guard-house, built in the lower floor (ground floor) of the King's Tower. The

Fig. 58. — Ramparts of the XVth century. — Section of the King's door.
(Restoration.)

large passage was closed, beyond the drawbridge, by two doors, one interior, protected by the portcullis, placed between the door and the flooring bank of the draw bridge, — the portcullis of the XVth century still exists, placed in its lateral grooves, — the other door opened outside on the street of the Town. After the doorkeeper had seen the comers and the contents of the carts the principal gate was externally shut by raising up the drawbridge, by means of the two lateral arms, pulled down from the interior of the passage — see fig. 58. The lateral drawbridge — of the postern — was equally worked from the interior and closed externally the postern by coming vertically against it in a recess built for that purpose.

On the exterior, the King's Gate, closed by its raised drawbridge, its portcullis and its doors, was protected by machicolations which adorn the higher part of the front and overlook the ditch now filled up which was on the base of the work.

The large opening of the door, shut by a very obtuse pointed arch is surmounted by a large pediment which still shows the traces of heraldic sculptures, laterally placed between two small buttresses surrounding the grooves of the arms of the drawbridge. It supports a row of small trifoiled series of arches, on which rest the principal brackets, with fine mouldings and higher machicolations which support an embattled and covered parapet joined to the battlement of the Towers and of the walls.

In front of the King's Gate, on the west, the exterior defences were completed, from 1425 to 1430 by the construction of the *Barbican* which still exists and, later, about 1530, by that of the *Avancée* before the entrance to the Town.

The *Barbican* is composed of a thick wall forming a very acute projecture towards the south-west, leaving between its front and the rock a very narrow space, and forming internally a parade ground in front of the Gate of the Town. The Gate and the Postern of the Barbican open on the west front of the curtain, flanked by a skew-back in the form of a fourth part of a circle, in front of the entrance and ending at the foot of the rock, inaccessible on this point. The walls are pierced with recesses for falconets and culverins, on the south, on the west and in the skew-back; the top of the walls is pierced with vertical loopholes and with loopholes provided with a circular sight in the middle for powder, known since the XIVth century, or for " the *hand-cannons* which were used during the whole time of the wars with the English. " (J. Quicherat, *Histoire du costume*, etc.)

The *Avancée* of the Barbican of the King's Gate taking the place of the palisade or wooden fence, which formerly was at the place where the Entrance to the Mount is actually was built by Gabriel du Puy about 1530. It offers on the south a front joined to the west curtain of the Barbican and before the entrance to this last work; at the west angle is a guard-house, on the left (the comer's left) of the Postern and of the principal Gate; this last was shut by a leaf opening externally in order to resist better every attempt to break through it or even to resist the pressure of the waters during the high tides. The pediment of the large Gate had surely some arms, — those of the king Francis the First without any doubt. Between the Gate and the Curtain, a loophole for a cannon in the wall protected the approaches of the Avancée. Lastly, in the court, a small embattled wall, leaning to the skew-back of the Barbican and communicating with the guard-house formed the second line of defences of the Gate of the *Barbican* when that of the *Avancée* was forced.

An illustration of the XVIIth century — fig. 59 — indicates in front of the *Avancée* a barrier inside of which stand the *forked gibbet* of the Abbey. We do not know any historical fact indicating that it was used for another purpose than to manifest the power of the Abbots and their seigneurial rights.

In the middle of that barrier a door shut by a panel rolling on an horizontal axe opened. The name of *Bavole Gate* given by some historians to the first entrance to the Town, comes very likely from this kind of en-

Fig. 39. — View of Mont Saint-Michel (according to the illustration by J. Peeters). — G. Merian, 1657.

closure, *bavole* instead of *bavoler* (to fly about), indicating a slight and easy to be managed fastening.

From the Avancée to the south west, where were the warehouses of the Abbey, the rock alone makes an insurmountable defence, its top is however edged by an embattled wall joined to the exterior circular roads, surrounding the Gardens of the Abbey on the south, the south west angle of which is surmounted by a watch tower.

At the foot of the rock, towards the west, outside the Enclosure stood the Edifices which belonged to the Abbey and included its warehouses, named the *Fanils* or *Fanis* (from *fanum*, hay, or better, from *fanile*, a place where the hay is stored). They were re-erected or rebuilt, in the beginning of the XIVth century, on the place of older constructions of the time of Robert de Torigni. There remain some traces of these edifices, on the west, on which stand the actual barracks built in 1818. The Entrance to the *Fanils* was protected by a Tower (*Fanils' Tower*, called by a corruption of language : *Stéphanie Tower*) flanking the south east angle and the base of which is still seen; it was in the XVIth century, preceded by a *ravelin* pierced by recesses, which still exists and forms a first court. The warehouses with their garrets, the abbatial oven, the stables, the cattle sheds, etc., extended on each side of the second interior court behind the gate protected by the Tower.

From this second court, horses and even carriages could ascend, by successive slopes to the table-land on which were the *Poulains*, which started from this plateau and ended at the basement of the Hostelry — see plan fig. 20. The exterior front of the *Fanils* was probably embattled and joined to the circular walls, also embattled, the ruins of which are seen and which were placed on the escarpments of the rock up to the inaccessible points. The exterior defences of that side of the Abbey were finished in the XVIth century by Gabriel du Puy, « a lieutenant of the King at the Mount. » He erected the Tower or Gabriel Bastillon, where the rock begins to be passable. Built in 1534, this work is composed of three floors of ranking batteries, pierced with embrasures of cannons, externally widened and covered with an annular vault falling very nearly in the middle on an enormous pier. At each of the three floors, the central pier is provided with a chimney-flue which was used for the ventilation of the battery, in order to take out rapidly the smoke of the powder; those chimney-flues necessarily met in a chimney, the shaft of which rose above the Platform, — before the Mill was built.

This higher platform was surrounded by a parapet pierced by slays, resting on machicolations which are only now a traditional decoration, except on the side of the rock, where they really protected the passage.

On this parapet, towards the west was a watch tower which is now used as a lighthouse. The Gate, or postern of the Gabriel Tower, built on the lower floor towards the rock and as much as possible concealed, was protected by a portcullis worked from the higher floor. Staircases make the diverse floors communicate together and end on the higher terrace, which is joined to the circular walls built in the rock. A postern built on the third floor of the Tower, allowed egress to the Fanils court, a necessary precaution to communicate internally with the adjacent defences or, if it was necessary, with the outside by the same way, for the lower floor was invaded by the water at spring tides.

In 1627, when Don Placide de Sarcus was Prior of the Abbey the Gabriel *Bastillon* was surmounted by a small tower in which a wind mill was established. The small tower was restored in 1880, after the purchase of the Tower by the Ministry of Public Instruction and Fine Arts, in 1876. The Ministry of public works paid one half of the cost.

After reading through the interesting military work about which we have just spoken, the visitor will be able, at low water, by following the slopes near the *Gabriel Bastillon* and going round the rocks on the west and on the south west to see Saint-Aubert's Chapel

13.

which rises on the side of the rock and to admire one of the most picturesque sites of Mont Saint-Michel.

Fig. 60. — Saint-Aubert's Chapel.

At last, to terminate suitably the excursion which the visitor will have made as complete as possible, if he has followed our indications, he must visit an establishment the name of which shows sufficiently its purpose and its use *i. e.* the *orphan asylum*, where the charity of those who, faithful to the old traditions, will be desirous to mark by a good action their passage at Mont Saint-Michel, may be exercised.

Fig. 61. — Mont Saint-Michel in Cornwall (England). Benedictine Abbey established by Edward the Confessor in honour of saint Michel.

TABLE OF ILLUSTRATIONS

Figures		Pages
	Title page.	3
1.	Frontispice.	2
2.	View of Mont Saint-Michel in 1878.	4
3.	Stamp of pilgrimage found at Mont Saint-Michel	6
4.	General view of the south front. — Condition in 1872. .	28
5.	— — Plan of Restoration .	29
6.	Scaffoldings for the works of Restoration	30
7.	General view of the west front	32
8.	— — north front.	34
9.	— — east front.	36
10.	King's Gate. — Perspective view.	38
11.	Street of the town.	41
12.	Interior of the town. — King's gate and Watch-tower. .	43
13.	Representations and moulds of Saint-Michel (stamps of pilgrimage).	44
14.	Representations and moulds of Saint-Michel (stamps of pilgrimage).	44
15.	Representations and moulds of Saint-Michel (stamps of pilgrimage).	45
16.	Representations and moulds of Saint-Michel (stamps of pilgrimage).	45

TABLE OF ILLUSTRATIONS

Figures		Pages
17.	Indented mould of a stamp of pilgrimage..........	46
18.	Proof in relief — —	46
19.	The Chatelet. — Entrance of the Abbey..........	48
20.	Ground plan of the Guard room. — 1st zone.......	50
21.	— of the lower church. — 2nd zone......	52
22.	— of the higher church. — 3rd zone......	54
23.	Fortified bridge in the court in front of the church....	58
24.	Transversal section of the Mount..............	62
25.	Longitudinal section.....................	63
26.	Edifice of Roger II.......................	65
27.	Gallery of the *Aquilon*	66
28.	Constructions of Robert de Torigni. — Plan of the basements.......	67
29.	Constructions of Robert de Torigni. — Ground plan of the Ambulatory.	68
30.	Constructions of Robert de Torigni. — Transverse section.........	70
31.	Plan of the church......................	72
32.	Plan of an arcade of the romanesque nave.........	74
33.	Transversal section of the romanesque Church......	76
34.	Longitudinal section —	77
35.	Chancel of the Church....................	79
36.	— — Section................	82
37.	North front of the Merveille.................	84
38.	Merveille. — Transversal section from the south to the north.......................	86
39.	Merveille. — Transversal section from the north to the south.......................	87
40.	Knights' hall........................	96
41.	Refectory...........................	99
42.	Cloister. — Plan of the north-east angle..........	101
43.	— View taken from the west gallery......	102
44.	— Sculptured angle tie, west gallery......	104
45.	— — — —	107

TABLE OF ILLUSTRATIONS

Figures		Pages
46.	Cloister. — Sculptured angle tie, east gallery.	108
47.	— — south —	109
48.	— — — —	110
49.	Plan of the exterior defences of the Abbey. — Barbican of the Chatelet, large flight of steps, etc.	124
50.	Large flight of steps, longitudinal section. — Condition in 1872.	127
51.	Large flight of steps, longitudinal section. — Restoration.	128
52.	East front of the Merveille and of the edifices forming the entrance to the Abbey	130
53.	Boulevard or east *Bastillon*.	135
54.	Ramparts of the XVth century. — Section of the Boucle Tower.	136
55.	Ramparts of the XVth century. — Boucle Tower.	137
56.	— — King's Gate	139
57.	Ramparts of the XVth century. — Plan of the entrance to the town.	140
58.	Remparts of the XVth century. — Section of the King's Gate.	142
59.	View of Mont Saint-Michel according to Mérian	146
60.	Saint-Aubert's chapel.	150
61.	Mont Saint-Michel in Cornwall (England).	151

TABLE OF CONTENTS

	Pages
Historical notice.	7
Itinerary.	31
General view.	33
The town.	40
The Abbey	49
Guards Room. — Belle-Chaise.	56
Abbatial buildings.	57
Church.	61
Substructures	64
Nave.	71
Chancel.	78
Lower church, called crypt of the large Pillars.	81
Merveille.	84
Almonry.	88
Cellar	90
Knights' hall.	94
Refectory.	98
Cloister.	101
Dormitory	113

Fortifications of the Merveille.	118
Fountain Saint-Aubert.	118

CHATELET 121

 Barbican of the Chatelet. — Large flight of steps on the north and Staircase on the south 123
 Large flight of steps and south Staircase 126

RAMPARTS. 131

Printing terminated
AT PARIS
On the twenty-first July eighteen hundred and eighty-three
by C. Marpon and E. Flammarion

FOR

ÉDOUARD CORROYER
ARCHITECT TO THE GOVERNMENT

LIBRAIRIE GÉNÉRALE DE L'ARCHITECTURE ET DES TRAVAUX PUBLICS

DUCHER ET CIE

51, Rue des Écoles, à Paris

✱

Médaille d'or à l'Exposition universelle
de 1878

EXTRAIT DU CATALOGUE

DESCRIPTION DE L'ABBAYE DU MONT SAINT-MICHEL ET DE SES ABORDS, par M. Édouard CORROYER, Architecte du Gouvernement. — 1 vol. gr. in-f°; 134 fig. et 6 eaux-fortes hors texte; grand plan en chromolithographie. — Prix, broché .... 12 fr.
Quelques exemplaires sur papier de Hollande. — Prix.... 20 fr.

REVUE GÉNÉRALE DE L'ARCHITECTURE ET DES TRAVAUX PUBLICS, journal des architectes, des archéologues, des ingénieurs, des entrepreneurs et des industriels, publié sous la direction de M. CÉSAR DALY. — 39e année. — 60 planches gravées ou chromolithographiées par année. — Abonnement annuel : Paris, 40 fr.; Départements, 45 fr.

LA SEMAINE DES CONSTRUCTEURS, journal hebdomadaire, *illustré*, des travaux publics et privés, sous la direction générale de M. CÉSAR DALY. — Rédacteur en chef : M. Paul PLANAT, ingénieur. — 6 années parues. — Abonnement annuel : Paris, 25 fr.; Départements, 27 fr.

LE RECUEIL D'ARCHITECTURE, publication mensuelle, sous la direction de MM. WULLIAM et FARGE, architectes, avec le concours des principaux architectes français et étrangers. — 10 années parues. — Abonnement annuel : Paris, 23 fr.; Départements, 25 fr.

CROQUIS D'ARCHITECTURE, publication mensuelle, par une Société d'architectes (*INTIME-CLUB*). — Compositions d'architecture. — Concours publics et de l'École des Beaux-Arts. — Dessins de voyages. — Œuvres exécutées. — 16 années parues. — Abonnement annuel : Paris, 18 fr.; Départements, 20 fr.

L'ARCHITECTURE PRIVÉE AU XIX⁰ SIÈCLE. — Nouvelles Maisons de Paris et des Environs.

1re *Série :* Étude spéciale de la distribution des plans et de la physionomie des ensembles. — 3 vol. in-fol., 236 planches et texte. Prix : en carton. . . . . 240 fr.

2e *Série :* Détails techniques et esthétiques. — Boutiques, Magasins, etc. — 3 vol. in-fol., 238 pl. et texte. — Prix : en carton. 240 fr

L'ARCHITECTURE FUNÉRAIRE. — Spécimens de Tombeaux, Mausolées, Chapelles funéraires, etc., etc. 1 vol. in-fol. — 120 planches, avec texte explicatif. — Prix : en carton. . . . . 150 fr.

PALAIS DE L'EXPOSITION UNIVERSELLE DE 1878, A PARIS, publié sous les auspices du Ministre de l'agriculture et du commerce. — I. *Palais du Champ-de-Mars.* — II. *Palais du Trocadéro.* — 2 vol., 93 planches. — Texte historique et descriptif. — Prix : en carton. . . . . 320 fr.

CONSTRUCTIONS EN BRIQUES. — La Brique ordinaire au point de vue décoratif, par J. LACROUX, architecte. — 1 vol. de 75 planches en couleurs. — Texte avec de nombreux dessins sur bois. — Prix : en carton. . . . . 125 fr.

MOTIFS D'ARCHITECTURE RUSSE. — 1 vol. gr. in-4. — 60 planches en couleurs. — Prix : en carton. . . . . 100 fr

LES HABITATIONS OUVRIÈRES EN TOUS PAYS, par ÉMILE MULLER. — 1 vol. grand in-8 de texte. — Album, en carton, de 70 planches. — Prix. . . . . 60 fr.

LES CHATEAUX HISTORIQUES. — *Anet,* par RODOLPHE PFNOR, architecte. — Le plus beau des édifices construits par PHILIBERT DELORME. — Nombreux documents inédits. — 1 vol. in-fol., 60 pl. avec texte illustré. — Prix : en carton. . . . . 150 fr.

Blois. — Ensembles et détails. — Extérieur : Détails d'Architecture et de Sculpture, etc. — Intérieur : Cheminées, Tentures, Plafonds, etc. — Restauration de M. FÉLIX DUBAN. — 1 vol. in-fol. — 60 pl., dont 35 photographies imprimées par un procédé qui les rend inaltérables, 12 (comptant pour 24) chromolithographies et 1 pl. gravée. — Texte par E. LE NAIL. — Prix : en carton, 180 fr.

Fontainebleau. — Extérieur et intérieur. — Vues d'ensemble. — Détails d'ornementation. — 30 belles photographies, grand in-folio. — Texte par E. LE NAIL. — Prix : en carton. . . . . 125 fr.

Pierrefonds, après la restauration de VIOLLET-LE-DUC. — Vues d'ensemble. — Détails extérieurs. — Décorations intérieures. —

12 belles photographies, grand in-fol. colombier. — Prix : en carton. . . . . 50 fr.

Chambord. — Vues d'ensemble. — Détails de Sculpture et d'Ornementation. — 12 belles photographies, grand in-folio. — Texte par AUGUSTE MILLOT. — Prix : en carton. . . . . 50 fr.

Coulanges-les-Royaux. — Cartouches et Caissons, relevés par OCTAVE DE ROCHEBRUNE. — 24 planches gravées à l'eau-forte. — 80 motifs différents. — Prix : en carton. . . . . 24 fr.

COURS DE CONSTRUCTION CIVILE, par P. PLANAT, rédacteur en chef de la *Semaine des Constructeurs*.

Construction et aménagement des Salles d'asile et des Maisons d'école. — 3 vol. grand in-4°. — Texte illustré de plus de 300 dessins; nombreux tableaux graphiques. — 244 planches en autographie. — Prix : en carton . . . . 100 fr.

Nouveau règlement pour la Construction et l'Ameublement des Écoles primaires, complété par les Nouvelles Instructions pour la construction des *Écoles maternelles et des Écoles primaires élémentaires.* — 96 pages illustrées. — Prix : broché. . . . . 4 fr.

Chauffage et ventilation des lieux habités. — 1 vol. grand in-8°, plus de 300 gravures. — Prix : broché. . 30 fr.

MOTIFS HISTORIQUES D'ARCHITECTURE ET DE SCULPTURE D'ORNEMENT. — Choix de fragments des monuments français du commencement du XVIe siècle jusqu'à la fin du XVIIIe.

1re *Série :* DÉTAILS EXTÉRIEURS. — 2 vol. in-fol. 198 pl. gravées. — Prix : en carton. 300 fr.

2e *Série :* DÉCORATIONS INTÉRIEURES. — 2 vol. in-fol. — 200 pl. gravées, ou en chromolithographie. — Prix : en carton. . . 300 fr.

LE NOUVEL OPÉRA DE PARIS, par M. CHARLES GARNIER, architecte, membre de l'Institut. — *Première partie.* — Comprenant la partie architecturale. — 2 vol. grand in-fol. — 100 planches, dont 20, comptant pour 40, en chromolithographie. — 2 volumes de texte. — Prix : les planches en carton, les 2 vol. de texte brochés. . . . . . 350 fr.

MONOGRAPHIE DE L'ANCIEN HOTEL DE VILLE DE PARIS, par VICTOR CALLIAT, architecte. — *Nouvelle édition sans texte et à prix considérablement réduit.* — 1 vol. in-4 colombier. — 89 pl. — Prix : en carton . . . . 80 fr.

MOBILIER D'ÉGLISES. — Spécimens choisis des divers styles depuis le XIe siècle jusqu'à nos jours.
   I. — **Ouvrages en pierre, en marbre et en fer.** — 1 vol. grand in-4. — 65 planches gravées. — Prix : en carton. 50 fr.
   II. — **Ouvrages en bois.** — 1 vol. grand in-4. — 65 planches gravées. — Prix : en carton . . . . 50 fr

VIGNOLE D'ARCHITECTURE, par THIOLLET, architecte. — Principes et études d'Architecture, d'après VIGNOLE, PALLADIO, etc. — 1 vol. grand in-4. — 30 planches gravées et texte. — Prix : broché. 7 fr.

LE PALAIS D'ULYSSE, A ITHAQUE. — *Architecture au temps d'Homère*, par M. CH. LUCAS. — 1 vol. in-8 illustré; 2 planches gravées. — Prix : broché. . . . . 5 fr.

LES ÉGLISES CIRCULAIRES D'ANGLETERRE, précédé de notes sur les temples ronds de la Grèce et de l'Italie et sur l'église du Saint-Sépulcre de Jérusalem. — *Seconde édition.* — Par M. CH. LUCAS, architecte. — 1 vol. grand in-8 de 64 pages, avec 5 plans et une vue intérieure. — Prix : broché. . . . . 4 fr.

L'ART DE BATIR CHEZ LES ROMAINS. — Étude théorique et pratique des diverses méthodes de construction des Romains, par M. A. CHOISY, ingénieur des ponts et chaussées. — 1 fort vol. in-folio de 27 pl. gravées. — 216 pages de texte. — Prix : en carton. . . 60 fr.

HISTOIRE GÉNÉRALE DE L'ARCHITECTURE, par DANIEL RAMÉE. — 2 vol. grand in-8; très nombreuses gravures. — Prix : broché. 30 fr.

L'ART DU XVIIIe SIÈCLE, par EDMOND et JULES DE GONCOURT. — *Seconde édition.* — 2 forts vol. grand in-8. — Édition de luxe. — Prix. . . . . 30 fr.

TYPES DE CONSTRUCTIONS RURALES (Culture mixte), par ÉMILE CARLIER, architecte. — 1 vol. grand in-4. — 30 planches gravées et texte. — Prix : en carton. . . . . 20 fr.

LE PAYSAGISTE. — Nouveau traité d'**Architecture de parcs et de Jardins** (École moderne), par M. LECOQ, architecte de Parcs et Jardins, inspecteur des Plantations de la Ville de Paris. — 1 vol. grand in-fol. — 32 planches gravées, plus de 100 plans de jardins variés. — Texte explicatif. — Prix : en carton . . . . . 65 fr.

L'ORNEMENT DES TISSUS, depuis les temps les plus reculés jusqu'à nos jours. — 1 vol. in-fol. (même format que l'*Ornement polychrome*). — 100 pl. *en couleurs, or et argent*, contenant près de 2,000 motifs. — Texte explicatif. — Prix : en carton. . . . . 150 fr.

LES TAPISSERIES DÉCORATIVES du Garde-Meuble (Mobilier national). — Fragments et motifs les plus beaux, par M. Ed. Guichard, architecte-décorateur. — Texte par M. Alfred Darcel. — 1 vol. in-fol. — 100 planches en héliogravure, dont un certain nombre en couleurs. — Prix : en carton.................. 200 fr.

LES TISSUS ANCIENS, reconstitués à l'aide du Costume, des Miniatures et de documents inédits, par M. Ed. Guichard, architecte-décorateur. — 1 vol. grand in-4, de 50 planches, avec texte. — Prix : en carton............................ 80 fr.

MÉLANGES D'ORNEMENTS de tous styles : Persan, Mauresque, Arabe, Grec, Gothique, Renaissance, xviie et xviiie siècles. — Composés et dessinés par M. E. Clerget. — 1 vol. in-fol. — 72 planches imprimées en couleurs. — Prix : cartonné................. 50 fr.

MOTIFS D'ORNEMENTS, pour Roses, Rosaces, Médaillons, Fonds et Panneaux, etc., dessinés par R. Pfnor, architecte. — 1 vol. gr. in-8. — 50 planches gravées. — Prix : en carton........... 40 fr.

DÉCORATIONS MURALES DU CHATEAU DE BLOIS, exécutées sous la direction de M. Félix Duban, membre de l'Institut. — 12 planches in-fol., en chromolithographie. — Prix : en carton...... 50 fr.

LA FLORE ORNEMENTALE, par M. Ruprich-Robert, architecte. — Étude de la Plante au point de vue de la Décoration et de l'Ornementation. — 1 vol. in-folio. — 150 planches avec texte. — Prix : en carton............................ 125 fr.

PARIS-SALON, par M. L. Énault. — Quatre années parues. La quatrième, 1882 : 2 vol. in-8. — Prix : broché, chacun..... 5 fr.

LE SALON DE 1882. — 1 vol. in-12 de 400 pages, 340 dessins, papier teinté. — Prix : broché..................... 2 fr. 50

L'ORNEMENT PAR LA NATURE, par M. H. Despois de Folleville. — 1 vol. in-4. — 100 pl. en autographie. — Prix : en carton... 25 fr.

L'HISTOIRE UNIVERSELLE PAR LE DESSIN. — Collection de dessins gravés sur le Mobilier, le Costume, les Armes, les Ustensiles, etc., des temps les plus anciens au xviiie siècle. — 1 vol. — 146 planches. — Plus de 1,000 dessins. — Prix : en carton......... 100 fr.

LA RELIURE ANCIENNE ET MODERNE. — Recueil de Reliures artistiques des xvie, xviie, xviiie et xixe siècles. — 2 vol. — 116 planches. — Texte, par Gustave Brunet. — Prix : en carton..... 53 fr.

ALBUMS DE FLEURS. — *Études et Compositions*, par Mmes Jumont.

I. — *Bouquets, Assiettes*, etc. — 30 pl. — Prix : en carton. 36 fr.

II. — *Fleurs naturelles.* — 24 planches. — Prix : en carton. 12 fr.

DÉCORATIONS MURALES DE POMPÉI, par Émile Presuhn, traduit de l'allemand par A. Giraud-Teulon. — Un beau vol. in-4, 51 pages de texte. — 24 planches en couleurs. — Prix : en carton. . 40 fr.

PEINTURES DECORATIVES du nouvel Opéra de Paris. — Un album de 20 photographies grand in-folio. — Prix : en carton. . . 70 fr.

GRAMMAIRE DE LA COULEUR. — Procédés pour préparer toutes les nuances et tous les tons dont un peintre décorateur peut avoir besoin, par M. Guichard. — 3 vol. in-8 oblong. — 700 planches en couleurs. — Prix : cartonné. . . . . 120 fr.

SPÉCIMENS DE LA DÉCORATION ET DE L'ORNEMENTATION AU XIXe SIÈCLE, par M. Liénard. — 1 vol. in-fol. de 125 pl. — Prix : en carton. . . . . 125 fr.

GRAMMAIRE ÉLÉMENTAIRE DU DESSIN, par M. L. Cernesson, architecte. — Ouvrage destiné à l'enseignement méthodique et progressif du *Dessin appliqué aux Arts*.

1re partie : **Dessin linéaire.** — 1 vol. grand in-4. — 30 planches gravées en taille-douce. — Texte explicatif, avec de nombreuses figures sur bois. — Prix de la première partie : en carton. 20 fr.

2e partie : **Cahiers des élèves.** — I. Cours élémentaire (6 à 9 ans). — 2 cahiers, 40 planches. — Prix. . . . . 2 fr.

II. Cours moyen (9 à 12 ans). — 2 cahiers, 40 pl. — Prix. . 2 fr.

III. Cours supérieur (12 à 14 ans). — 1er cahier, 20 pl. — Prix. 1 fr.

     —   —   2e cahier, 20 pl. avec teintes. Prix. . . . . 3 fr.

V. Cahier complémentaire des Cours moyen et supérieur. — Emploi des couleurs. — 10 pl. en chromolithographie. — Prix. . 5 fr.

LE COSTUME HISTORIQUE, par M. A. Racinet, architecte, auteur de *l'Ornement polychrome*. — 500 planches, dont 300 en couleurs, or et argent, et 200 en camaïeu, avec des notices explicatives. — L'ouvrage sera publié en 20 livraisons contenant chacune 15 planches en couleurs et 10 en camaïeu : *les treize premières livraisons sont en vente*.

— Prix de la livraison : édition de luxe à petites marges. . 12 fr.

     —   —   à grandes marges. 25 fr.

LA PEINTURE MURALE DÉCORATIVE, dans le style du Moyen âge, par MM. W. et G. AUDSLEY, membre de l'Institut royal des Architectes britanniques. — 1 vol. in-4. — 36 planches en couleurs et or. — Notices explicatives. — Prix : en carton. . . . . 50 fr.

PEINTURE DÉCORATIVE. — Panneaux exécutés dans les ateliers de M. ARTHUR MARTIN, et reproduits par la photographie. — Album de 12 planches. — Prix : en carton . . . . 30 fr.

LES ORNEMANISTES DU XIXᵉ SIÈCLE. — Compositions d'ornements, par FEUCHÈRE, LIÉNARD, PRIGNOT, POTERLET. RIESTER, etc. — 1 vol. grand in-4 colombier. — 45 pl. gravées. — Prix : en carton. 40 fr.

DOCUMENTS ET ŒUVRES D'ART du xᵉ au xviiᵉ siècle, tirés des collections les plus célèbres. — 1 vol. grand in-folio. — 30 planches gravées. — Prix : en carton. . . . . 50 fr.

COURS ÉLÉMENTAIRE DE PAYSAGE AU FUSAIN, par KARL ROBERT, imprimé par LEMERCIER et Cᵉ. — 1 fort vol. grand in-4 de 30 pl. — Texte explicatif. — Prix : en carton toile. . . . . 30 fr.

GRAMMAIRE DE L'ORNEMENT JAPONAIS, par M. THOMAS-W. CUTLER, membre de l'Institut royal des Architectes britanniques. — 1 beau volume. — 58 planches tirées en couleurs. — Texte en anglais. — Prix : richement cartonné. . . . . 75 fr.

COURS D'AQUARELLE, par EUGÈNE CICÉRI. — Cours complet en vingt-cinq leçons progressives, d'après une méthode toute nouvelle. — Album de 48 planches, avec texte. — Prix : en carton. . . 40 fr.

LE JUGEMENT DERNIER, peint par MICHEL-ANGE BUONAROTTI, dans la chapelle Sixtine, à Rome. — Album de 17 planches grand in-folio, gravées par THANUS PIROLI. — Texte. — Prix : en carton. . . 20 fr.

RECUEIL D'ORNEMENTS (Style russo-byzantin). par L.-L. BALACHOFF, artiste russe. — Lithographié par S.-N. BASCHOFF, éditeur, à Moscou. — 1 album gr. in-4. — 54 pl. — Prix : en carton. 25 fr.

AMEUBLEMENT PRATIQUE. — Choix de modèles de Meubles simples de tous styles, par TH. MERLIN, dessinateur. — 1 vol. grand in-4. — 50 pl. en lithographie. — Prix : en carton. . . . . 30 fr.

DICTIONNAIRE DU TAPISSIER. — Histoire de l'Ameublement français, depuis les temps les plus anciens jusqu'à nos jours, par J. DEVILLE. — 2 vol. grand in-4°. — 500 pages de texte. — 110 planches tirées en couleurs. — Prix : en carton. . . . . 80 fr.

L'AMEUBLEMENT MODERNE, par MM. PRIGNOT, LIÉNARD, etc. — Collection variée de modèles de tous les styles pour Meubles divers.

— 1 vol. — 120 planches en lithographie et 24 grandes feuilles de détails d'exécution. — Prix. . . . . 120 fr.

ALBUMS DU PEINTRE EN BATIMENT. — Travaux élémentaires, par M. N. GLAISE, peintre. — Les Bois et les Marbres, par M. EUGÈNE BERTHELON.

1re *Série*. — **Filage**. Ornements à plat, Bordures, Frises. — — 1 vol. in-folio. — 30 pl. en couleurs. — Prix : en carton. . 50 fr.

2e *Série*. — **Bois et Marbres**. — Lettres, Filage, etc. — 1 vol. in-fol. — 30 pl. en couleurs. — Texte. — Prix : en carton. . 75 fr.

3e *Série*. — **Décors et Attributs**. — Cartouches, Lettre ornées, Bronze, Trophées, etc. — 1 vol. in-folio. — 30 planches couleurs. — Texte. — Prix : en carton. . . . . 75 .

4e *Série*. — **Modèles de lettres**, sur 20 tons de fonds diffé rents. — 20 alphabets. — 1 vol. in-folio. — 20 planches en couleurs. — Texte. — Prix : en carton. . . . . 30 fr.

ALBUM DE L'ORNEMENTATION PRATIQUE, par une réunion d'ornemanistes et de sculpteurs. — Cheminées, Chapiteaux, Clefs, Consoles, etc. — 2 beaux vol. grand in-4. de 110 photographies. — Prix : en carton. . . . . 150 fr.

ALBUM DE LA DÉCORATION USUELLE, faisant suite à l'album de l'*Ornementation pratique*. — 2 volumes grand in-4. — 110 photographies. — Prix : en carton. . . . . 150 fr.

L'ART ET L'INDUSTRIE, organe du Progrès dans toutes les branches de l'Industrie artistique. — 12 livraisons par an. — Chacune se compose de six planches gravées, d'une planche en couleurs et de deux pages de texte. — *Septième année* (1883).

    Abonnement annuel : Paris. . . . . 18 fr.
    — Départements. . . . 20 fr.

L'ART PRATIQUE. — Recueil de documents choisis dans les ouvrages des grands maîtres français, italiens, etc. — 12 livraisons de chacune 12 planches par année. — *Cinquième année* (1883).

    Abonnement annuel : Paris. . . . . 18 fr.
    — Départements. . . . 20 fr.

MAGASIN DES ARTS ET DE L'INDUSTRIE. — *Ouvrage complet.* Magnifique collection de modèles et de spécimens de l'*Art industriel* moderne de tous les pays et sous toutes ses formes. — Prix : en carton. . . . . 120 fr.

STATUES DÉCORATIVES du nouvel Opéra de Paris. — 1 volume de 35 photographies grand in-folio. — Prix : carton. . . . . 90 fr.

LE MOBILIER DE LA COURONNE et des grandes collections, par R. Pfnor, architecte. — 3 vol. in-fol., contenant chacun 40 planches gravées ou grands dessins au crayon, 10 grandes feuilles de détails ou épures d'exécution, et un texte. — Prix : en carton... 120 fr.

MATÉRIAUX ET DOCUMENTS D'ARCHITECTURE ET DE SCULPTURE, classés par ordre alphabétique, par M. Raguenet, architecte. — Une livraison par mois, de 8 pages in-4. — Environ 350 motifs par année. — Onze années parues. — Prix : Abonnement courant (Paris et départements)................. 12 fr.

MOTIFS DIVERS DE SERRURERIE. Extrait de la *Revue générale de l'Architecture* et des divers ouvrages de M. César Daly.

1re *Partie.* — **Serrurerie ancienne et Ferronerie.** — Album de 35 planches gravées. — Prix : en carton..... 25 fr.

2e *Partie.* — **Serrurerie moderne.** — Album de 30 planches gravées. — Prix : en carton................. 25 fr.

LE CHARPENTIER-SERRURIER AU XIXe SIÈCLE. — Constructions en fer et en bois. — Publié sous le patronage de M. Alphand, directeur des travaux de Paris, par J. Ferrand, architecte. — Album de 100 planches tirées en diverses couleurs et accompagnées d'un texte, Prix : en carton..................... 60 fr.

RECUEIL PRATIQUE DE CHARPENTE, par MM. Gateuil et Bezancenet, architectes. — Choix de modèles variés. — 1 vol. in-4. — 100 pl. tirées en plusieurs couleurs. — Prix : en carton.... 30 fr.

DICTIONNAIRE PRATIQUE DU SERRURIER, par M. A. Husson. — 1 vol. in-12. — Prix : broché.................. 3 fr.

CHARPENTES EN BOIS. — Album renfermant divers types de Combles, Halles, Hangars, Ponts, Estacades, Échafaudages et Étayements, etc., par M. Loyau, ingénieur. — Atlas in-4 de 120 planches. — Prix................................. 25 fr.

DICTIONNAIRE DES OUVRIERS EN BATIMENT, par M. Jossier. — 1 fort vol. grand in-8. — Prix : broché............ 7 fr. 50

L'ART DE LA MENUISERIE, par Roubo. — *Nouvelle édition,* par un Comité d'architectes, d'entrepreneurs de menuiserie, de chefs d'atelier, de professeurs de trait, etc. — Art du Trait, Menuiserie dormante, Menuiserie du bâtiment, etc. — 1 fort volume de texte in-8 et un album de 108 planches, grand in-4. — Prix : le volume de texte broché, l'album en carton............. 30 fr.

TARIF DE FILAGE, par N. Glaise, peintre, auteur de l'*Album du*

Peintre en Bâtiment. — Indispensable aux architectes, aux vérificateurs, aux entrepreneurs de peinture, etc. — Brochure in-16, avec 1 planche gravée, donnant les profils de toutes les moulures les plus généralement employées dans la peinture décorative. — — Prix.. . . . . 1 fr. 25

COURS DE CONSTRUCTION, par le major du génie N. DE VOS. — Connaissance des matériaux; leur Résistance. — 2 vol. grand in-8. — Nombreuses figures dans le texte. — Prix : les 2 vol. br., 40 fr.

LA TECHNOLOGIE DU BATIMENT, par TH. CHATEAU. — *Nouvelle édition*. — Étude de tous les matériaux employés dans les constructions depuis leur fondation jusques et y compris leur décoration. — 2 forts vol., avec bois intercalés. — Carte géologique de la France en couleurs. — Prix : broché. 30 fr.

DE L'HUMIDITÉ DANS LES CONSTRUCTIONS ET DES MOYENS DE S'EN GARANTIR, par M. PHILIPPE. — 2ᵉ édition, illustrée. — Prix : broché. . . . . 6 fr.

DANGERS, AU POINT DE VUE SANITAIRE, DES MAISONS MAL CONSTRUITES, par le docteur PRIDGIN TEALE. Traduit de l'anglais, par M. KIRK, avec une préface de M. SIEGFRIED, maire du Havre.— 1 vol. in-8, de 155 pages et 67 planches, cartonné à l'anglaise. — Prix. . . . . 12 fr. 50

ASSAINISSEMENT DE PARIS. — Suppression complète de la Vidange. — Le système diviseur appliqué à l'égout, par M. EUG. MIOTAT, Architecte-Voyer de la ville de Paris. Extrait de la *Semaine des Constructeurs*. — Plaquette in-8, de 41 pages, avec de nombreux bois dans le texte. — Prix : broché. . . . . 2 fr. 50

ASSAINISSEMENT DES ÉGOUTS ET DES HABITATIONS, par M. E. MIOTAT, architecte expert. — Plaquette, 48 pages et 11 bois dans le texte. — Prix. . . . . 3 fr.

LA QUESTION DU FEU DANS LES THÉATRES, par M. CHENEVIER. — Brochure de 68 pages grand in-8. — Prix : broché. . . . . . . 3 fr.

TRAITÉ DES PARATONNERRES, par M. CALLAUD. — 1 vol. grand in-8, nombreuses gravures. — Prix broché.. . . . . 7 fr. 50

TRAITÉ DE LA LÉGISLATION ET DE L'ADMINISTRATION DE LA VOIRIE URBAINE, par M. A. DES CILLEULS. — 1 vol. grand in-8, de 700 pages. — Prix : broché. . . . . 10 fr.

HISTOIRE DE LA LÉGISLATION DES TRAVAUX PUBLICS, par M. MALAPERT, avocat. — 1 vol. — Prix : broché. . . . . 10 fr.

ÉTUDE THÉORIQUE ET PRATIQUE SUR LES MURS DE SOUTÈNEMENT, par M. Dubosque. — 1 vol. grand in-8, 9 planches et 74 gravures. — Prix : broché.................... 10 fr.

MANUEL DES ENTREPRENEURS. — Ordonnances et règlements de police, par M. Desplanques. — 2 vol. grand in-8 de 448 pages. — Prix.................................. 11 fr.

MANUEL DES LOIS DU BATIMENT, élaboré par la Société centrale des Architectes, voté en Assemblée générale. — *Nouvelle édition*, entièrement refondue et considérablement augmentée. — 5 volumes gr. in-8, imprimé sur beau et fort papier. — Prix : brochés, 40 fr.; cartonnés à l'anglaise, avec fer spécial sur le plat, 45 fr.; relié demi-maroquin, 52 fr. — Ajouter 3 fr. 50 pour recevoir *franco* en province.

TRAITÉ DES RÉPARATIONS (Lois du Bâtiment), par A. Le Bègue, architecte expert près les tribunaux. — Réparations locatives : Gros entretien. — Réparations usufruitières : Grosses réparations. — Droits et obligations du Locataire preneur. — Charges du bailleur, etc. — *Troisième édition*, soigneusement revue par l'auteur et notablement augmentée. — 1 vol. gr. in-8. — Prix : broché. 5 fr.

CARNET DU CONDUCTEUR DE TRAVAUX. — Recueil de formules, tables, renseignements pratiques, par F. Vasselon, ingénieur civil. — *Seconde édition*. — 1 vol. contenant plus de 3,000 formules et 350 figures intercalées dans le texte. — Prix : relié en forme de carnet-portefeuille........................ 7 fr. 25

SÉRIE OFFICIELLE DES PRIX DE RÈGLEMENT DE LA VILLE DE PARIS. — *Nouvelle édition simplifiée*. — La série complète avec les sous-détails. — Prix................... 30 fr.
La série dite de poche. — Prix : cartonné......... 11 fr.

SÉRIE DE PRIX APPLICABLES AUX TRAVAUX DE TREILLAGES ET RUSTIQUE, établie par la Chambre syndicale des entrepreneurs de treillages. — Prix : broché.................. 4 fr.
Ce prix est réduit à 2 fr. pour les acheteurs de la Série officielle.

SÉRIE DE PRIX POUR LE RÈGLEMENT NORMAL DES TRAVAUX DE SERRURERIE. — Charpentes métalliques, paratonnerres, sonneries, porte-voix, etc., avec de nombreux renseignements pour l'établissement des devis, par M. H. de Persin. — 1 vol. format de poche, de 170 pages. — Prix : cartonné................. 6 fr.

COLLECTION DES OUVRAGES DE M. MASSELIN, entrepreneur de travaux publics, savoir :

Les Honoraires des Architectes, en matière de travaux publics et particuliers. — 1 vol. de 264 pages. — Prix. 12 fr.

La Responsabilité des Architectes et des Entrepreneurs. — *Seconde édition.* — 1 vol. de 362 pages. — Prix. . . . . 12 fr.

Les Devis dépassés et Travaux supplémentaires. — 1 vol. in-8 de 166 pages. — Prix. . . . . 6 fr.

Les Locations immobilières : Obligations des propriétaires. — 1 vol. — Prix. . . . . 10 fr.

Les Murs mitoyens. — *Troisième édition.* — 1 vol., 4 suppléments et un album de figures. — Prix. . . . . 22 fr.

Le Dictionnaire du Métré. — Commentaire sur la série de prix de la Ville de Paris. — *Nouvelle édition.* — 1 vol. de 344 pages et 11 planches. — Prix. 10 fr.

Formules de statuts pour la constitution des Sociétés anonymes. — Prix : par 5 ex. à la fois. . . . . 20 fr.

Devis descriptifs et **Cahier des charges.**

Carnets-contrôles à l'usage des entrepreneurs.

(*Demander les prospectus spéciaux.*)

LE CONSEILLER DES PROPRIÉTAIRES ET DES LOCATAIRES, par ÉMILE BLANCHARD, architecte. — 1 vol. grand in-8, de 216 pages. — Prix. . . . . 6 fr.

TARIF DE CUBAGE DES BOIS EN GRUME, par M. ADRIAN. — 1 vol. in-16 de 170 pages. — Prix : broché. . . . . 2 fr. 50

MÉMENTO DU MÉTREUR-VÉRIFICATEUR, par M. HUSSON. — 4ᵉ édition. — Prix. . . . . 1 fr. 25

CHAUFFAGE ET VENTILATION DES LIEUX HABITÉS, par M. P. PLANAT. — 1 vol. gr. in-8, plus de 300 gravures. — Prix : broché. 30 fr.

TRAITÉ DE COMPTABILITÉ A L'USAGE DES ENTREPRENEURS, par M. DUGUÉ, ingénieur. — 1 vol. in-8. — Prix : broché. . . . . . 4 fr.

*

Le Catalogue est envoyé franco contre demande.

*

Les prix portés sur ce Catalogue sont spéciaux à la France. Pour l'étranger, il y a les frais en sus.

www.ingramcontent.com/pod-product-compliance
Lightning Source LLC
Chambersburg PA
CBHW032158160426
43197CB00008B/974